PROPERTY RIGHTS IN THE
EIGHTH-CENTURY PROPHETS

SOCIETY
OF BIBLICAL
LITERATURE

DISSERTATION SERIES

J. J. M. Roberts, Old Testament Editor
Charles Talbert, New Testament Editor

Number 106

PROPERTY RIGHTS IN THE
EIGHTH-CENTURY PROPHETS

by
John Andrew Dearman

John Andrew Dearman

PROPERTY RIGHTS IN THE EIGHTH-CENTURY PROPHETS
The Conflict and its Background

Scholars Press
Atlanta, Georgia

PROPERTY RIGHTS IN THE EIGHTH-CENTURY PROPHETS

John Andrew Dearman

Library of Congress Cataloging-in-Publication Data

Dearman, John Andrew.
  Property rights in the eighth-century prophets.

  (Dissertation series / Society of Biblical
Literature ; no. 106
  Bibliography: p.
  1. Property.   2. Bible.   Old Testament.
Prophets—Criticism, interpretation, etc.
3. Property rights—Biblical teaching.   I. Title.
II. Series: Dissertation series (Society of Biblical
Literature) ; no. 106.
HB701.D4 1987   330'.17   87-28511
ISBN 1-55540-192-9 (alk. paper)
ISBN 1-55540-195-3 (pbk. : alk. paper)

Printed in the United States of America
on acid-free paper

Contents

Preface

With editing and minor changes this volume is the author's 1981 Emory dissertation completed under the direction of Professor John H. Hayes. Since the dissertation series precludes changes in references for updating, perhaps I might be permitted a reference to a paper where I provide some update to the subject matter and bibliography: "Prophecy, Property and Politics," *SBLSP* (ed. Kent Harold Richards; Chico: Scholars Press, 1984) 385-97.

I am grateful to a number of persons for their support and encouragement. My family comes first to mind and for them I am eternally grateful. In recent months my employer, Austin Presbyterian Theological Seminary, has provided both financial support and encouragement in preparing the manuscript for publication. The initial work would never have been completed were it not for the advice and constructive criticism of my teachers at Emory. To John Hayes in particular I offer thanks to one who embodies the love of learning. Even two friends from Brigham Young University whom I have never met, Professor David F. Wright and Mr. Charles D. Bush, provided me with a Near Eastern font for typing without which I could not have prepared the manuscript properly. I am thankful for the current editors and the staff at Scholars Press for the publication of this work. As always, my chief thanks goes to Kathy; and as with the original dissertation, this volume is also dedicated to her.

Epiphany, 1988.

Abbreviations

ABR	*Australian Biblical Review*
AJSL	*American Journal of Semitic Languages and Literature*
ANET	*Ancient Near Eastern Texts* (ed. J. B. Pritchard)
ARM	*Archives royales de Mari*
BA	*Biblical Archaeologist*
BAR	*Biblical Archaeology Review*
BASOR	*Bulletin of the American Schools of Oriental Research*
BHS	*Biblia Hebraica Stuttgartensia*
Bib	*Biblica*
Bi Or	*Bibliotheca Orientalis*
CBQ	*Catholic Biblical Quarterly*
DtrH	Deuteronomistic History/Historian
EI	*Eretz Israel*
EvT	*Evangelische Theologie*
Exp Tim	*Expository Times*
HTR	*Harvard Theological Review*
HUCA	*Hebrew Union College Annual*
IDBS	*Interpreter's Dictionary of the Bible, Supplementary Volume*
IEJ	*Israel Exploration Journal*

IOS	*Israel Oriental Studies*
JAAR	*Journal of the American Academy of Religion*
JAOS	*Journal of the American Oriental Society*
JBL	*Journal of Biblical Literature*
JESHO	*Journal of the Economic and Social History of the Orient*
JNES	*Journal of Near Eastern Studies*
JQR	*Jewish Quarterly Review*
JR	*Journal of Religion*
JSOT	*Journal for the Study of the Old Testament*
KAI	*Kanaanäische und aramäische Inschriften* (ed. H. Donner and W. Röllig)
KB	*Hebräische und aramäische Lexikon zum Alten Testament* (L. Köhler and W. Baumgartner)
KD	*Kerygma und Dogma*
Kl Schr	*Kleine Schriften zur Geschichte des Volkes Israel* (A. Alt)
LXX	Septuagint
MT	Masoretic Text
NZSyTh	*Neue Zeitschrift für Systematische Theologie*
Or	*Orientalia*
Or Ant	*Oriens Antiquus*
OTS	*Oudtestamentische Studiën*

PEQ   *Palestine Exploration Quarterly*

RB   *Revue Biblique*

RStR   *Religious Studies Review*

SBLSP   *Society of Biblical Literature Seminar Papers*

ST   *Studia Theologica*

TA   *Tel Aviv*

UF   *Ugaritische Forshungen*

VT   *Vetus Testamentum*

VTSup   *Vetus Testamentum Supplements*

ZAW   *Zeitschrift für die alttestamentliche Wissenschaft*

ZDPV   *Zeitschrift des deutschen Palastina-Vereins*

Introduction

This dissertation is an investigation of the references to property rights in the eighth century prophetical literature and an attempt to understand these references in the socio-economic context of Israel's history.[1] Eighth-century prophecy naturally includes the books of Amos, Hosea, Isaiah and Micah, or those sections in them which can be assigned with reasonable certainty to the eighth century. Terms such as "property" or "rights" deserve further clarification. Property is defined as an object or entity which a person owns, legally possesses or over which he/she has the power of disposal. The following definition of a "right" used in a recent study of casuistic law is also applicable to the present study:

> A primary right is an entitlement to be or do something. Others owe duties to one's right. The right is qualified by corresponding duties. Primary rights and duties exist in themselves prior to any breach of (those, J. A. D.) rights.[2]

There are two reasons for adopting this definition of a right. The first is that rights can have their basis in statutory law, custom or even ethics. Property laws in ancient Israel are at best imperfectly known and to limit the investigation to what has been surmised or defined as law would be too restrictive. The second reason comes from the Hebrew Bible. In at least three texts (1 Sam 8:9; Jer 32:7; Isa 10:2), reference is made to someone's right *(mišpāṭ)* with regard to the possession and disposal of property. A property right, then, is an entitlement to own, possess or dispose of property and the obligation to perform any duties associated with (or that accrue to) such a right.

---

[1]   The present study is primarily concerned with civil property rights and not the rights or duties associated with presenting offerings (property) for cultic worship. For these latter references in the prophetical literature, see, R. J. Thompson, *Penitence and Sacrifice in Early Israel Outside the Levitical Law* (Leiden: E. J. Brill, 1963) 161-82.

[2]   D. Patrick, "Casuistic Law Governing Primary Rights and Duties," *JBL* 92 (1973) 181. What Patrick calls "primary rights" are called simply "rights" in the present work.

In the prophetical texts there is no discussion of property rights for their own sake. Most references to them occur in the midst of perceived conflict and accusations. Thus the investigation is inevitably thrust into the broader subject of prophecy and social criticism. In fact, any discussion of the topic defined above as property rights usually comes in scholarly literature dealing with this broader subject. In order to appreciate this factor, it is necessary to make a brief survey of some studies related to the topic of prophecy and social criticism. The survey is intended as a brief overview of the broader subject of prophecy and social criticism, and also as a prolegomenon to the more restricted topic of the dissertation. The following survey is selective and intended to highlight several issues dealt with in the dissertation. The survey begins by sketching two broad trends in the study of prophecy. Within these trends several approaches to the subject of prophecy and social criticism are briefly presented. Next the works of a few individual scholars are presented in more detail, especially as they relate to the specific topic of property rights. An outline of the dissertation concludes the introduction.

History of Research

The interpretation of the prophets underwent substantial change in the nineteenth century. Progress in the historical-critical study of the Bible led to the rejection of the then common view that the prophets were exponents of Mosaic law and/or predictors of the future. Scholars such as Duhm,[3] Kuenen,[4] and Wellhausen[5] argued that the early writing prophets were innovators and individualists who represented the pinnacle of Israel's religious development. The great insight and accomplishment of the prophets were their emphases on the moral basis of the relationship between YHWH and his people. In their social

---

[3]   B. Duhm, *Die Theologie der Propheten als Grundlage für die innere Entwicklungsgeschichte der Israelitischen Religion* (Bonn: Adolph Marcus, 1875).

[4]   A. Kuenen, *The Prophets and Prophecy in Israel* (London: Longmans, Green & Co., 1877); the Dutch original was published in 1875.

[5]   J. Wellhausen, *Israelitische und Judische Geschichte* (Berlin: de Gruyter, 1958) 122-32; the first edition was published in 1878.

criticism, the prophets depended primarily on the natural moral law[6] and not on a written code. They were considered the founders of ethical monotheism.[7] The influence of the prophets was seen in the social concerns reflected in the laws of Deuteronomy and the "H" and "P" sources of the Pentateuch.

Wellhausen was careful to say, however, that these prophets were not preaching anything new but in a forceful manner only what was traditional among the people.[8] Yet this (necessary) qualification did not prevent many scholars who followed from developing the emphasis on the new element in the prophetic preaching. A striking example of this general tendency is the statement by W. R. Harper concerning Amos: "There were probably not fifty people in Northern Israel who could understand him."[9]

This line of scholarship emphasized the development and change within Israel's history and made this development a background for the social conflict witnessed in the prophetic writings. Specifically, it was argued that Israelite society developed from nomadic or seminomadic origins to a monarchical, commercial state. Wellhausen, who advocated this general view, summed it up by stating: "Der Handel war lange nur von den kanaanitischen Stadten betrieben, so dass der Name Kanaanit sogar geradezu zur Bezeichnung eines Handlers diente. Jetzt aber trat Israel in Kanaans Fusstapfen, zum Leidwesen der Propheten."[10]

A consequence of this approach to the prophets was a tendency to paint the background to the prophetic social critique with broad strokes. Their social critique was based on "broad humanitarian ideals"[11] or the background to their ministry was described as "the rich grew richer and

---

6 R. Oden, "Hermeneutics and Historiography: Germany and America," *SBLSP* (ed. P. Achtemeier; Chico: Scholars Press, 1980) 135-58, esp. 140-41, points out that the apprehension of a moral world as the goal of history was an important theme in nineteenth century German historical scholarship.

7 Kuenen, *Prophets,* 589-91; Wellhausen, *Geschichte,* 108.

8 Wellhausen, *Geschichte,* 107.

9 W. R. Harper, *Amos and Hosea* (ICC; New York: C. Scribner's Sons, 1905). cxxx.

10 Wellhausen, *Geschichte,* 82-3.

11 J. M. Powis Smith, *The Prophets and Their Times* (Chicago: University of Chicago Press, 1940) 64.

more powerful, the poor grew poorer."[12] The prophets were considered reformers who advocated, in part, liberal political views which frequently paralleled those held by their modern interpreters. On the American scene at least, this correlation between modern interpreter and ancient prophet is unmistakable in the reference (in 1934!) to the prophets and the "New Deal" by W. C. Graham.[13]

Another major impulse or trend for research came in the recognition that the prophetical message employed many forms of speech from various social settings.[14] This emphasis on the forms of the prophetic message led to the investigation of the traditions upon which the message might be based. Prophetic traditions and speech forms were traced to cultic texts, sacral or covenant law, a wisdom ethos, temple-entrance liturgies, law court procedures, and vision and theophany reports.[15] In evaluating the prophetic social critique, the emphasis of scholarship was no longer on the prophets as innovators and individualists but upon the various traditions employed by the prophets to make their point. Von Rad's often-used volume on the prophets is a noteworthy example of this trend, especially in his efforts to present the prophets as creative reinterpreters of older Yahwistic traditions.[16]

As noted previously, the references in the prophetic literature to property rights form a part of the prophets' more general and fundamental social critique. There are several representative

---

[12]   A. F. Kirkpatrick, *Doctrine of the Prophets* (London: Macmillan & Co., 1932) 155. See Powis Smith, *Prophets*, 59, for an almost identical statement.

[13]   W. C. Graham, *The Prophets and Israel's Culture* (Chicago: University of Chicago Press, 1934) 40.

[14]   The reference is to the application of form-criticism to biblical texts. For the prophetical literature, see C. Westermann, *Basic Forms of Prophetic Speech* (Philadelphia: Westminster Press, 1967); J. H. Hayes, "The History of the Form-Critical Study of Prophecy," *SBLP* (ed. G. MacRae; Missoula: Scholars Press, 1973), 1. 60-99.

[15]   In addition to the bibliography mentioned in note 14, see E. March, "Prophecy," *Old Testament Form Criticism* (TUMSR 2; ed. J. H. Hayes, San Antonio: Trinity University Press, 1974) 141-78.

[16]   See volume two of his *Old Testament Theology* (New York: Harper & Row, 1965).

approaches[17] (below) for understanding this critique. Each of these representative positions provides an avenue of approach that can illumine some facet of prophecy and social criticism and the references to property rights which are often found in that context. Bibliographic citations in the notes are meant to be representative not exhaustive.

(1) The prophets perceived a *moral order* which was universal in scope and in which the consciousness of the prophet was deeply imbued. No revealed law was necessary to discern the corruptness of certain social institutions or the need for social change. The only requirement was the conscience of an individual who was further enlightened by the apprehension of YHWH's moral character.[18]

(2) A second approach sees the prophets as *preachers of the divine law*, proceeding on the basis of a correspondence between certain ethical requirements in the legal corpora of the Pentateuch and the prophetic accusations. This view is not so much a return to the pre-critical views about the prophets as Moses' interpreters, though the ideal or actuality of a Mosaic office may have influenced the work of the prophets,[19] as a recognition of substantial overlap between the concerns of the prophets and the compilers of the legal traditions. Also involved is a more positive view of "law," both with regard to its function and its chronological priority to classical prophecy, than that held by either Duhm or Wellhausen. The divine law upon which the prophets depended could have its basis in either the tribal league (amphictyony) and/or proclamation in the cult.[20]

---

17   See K. Koch, "Die Entstehung der sozialen Kritik bei den Profeten," *Probleme biblischer Theologie*, (ed. H. W. Wolff; München: Chr. Kaiser, 1971) 239-42, for a similar survey. The present survey is arranged differently and refers to more English speaking scholars than Koch.

18   In addition to the scholars mentioned in notes 3-5, 11, see also C. F. Whitley, *The Prophetic Achievement* (Leiden: E. J. Brill, 1963).

19   H. G. Reventlow, *Das Amt der Propheten bei Amos* (FRLANT 80; Göttingen: Vandenhoeck & Ruprecht, 1962).

20   W. Zimmerli, *The Law and the Prophets* (Oxford: Basil Blackwell, 1965); E. Würthwein, "*Amos Studien,*" *ZAW* 62 (1950) 47-52; R. Bach, "Gottesrecht und weltliches Recht in der Verkündigung des Propheten Amos," *Festschrift fur Gunther Dehn* (ed. W. Schneemelcher; Neukirchen-Vluyn: Neukirchener Verlag, 1957) 23-34; W. Beyerlin, *Die*

(3) A third approach has as its common denominator a stress on a *societal ideal* upon which the prophets drew for their social critique. One common view emphasizes the characterization of Israel as the "people of God," an elect people whose distinctive Israelite values were gradually corrupted in the postsettlement period by the growing power of the monarchy, commercialism, and the native Canaanite population.[21]   A further development within this category is the tendency to see in the prophetic preaching an assumption of *utopian ideals*. This view generally concluded that the powerful figures verbally attacked by the prophets could make little practical use of their words in either the social or political realm. The prophets relied on an older conception of Yahwistic morality based on an idealization of the past.[22]   A third, similar interpretation concluded the prophetic ideals were based on the conception of a previous "ideal" *nomadic period* or at least an analogous cultural matrix. The prophets then mediated an old tribal, brotherly ethic to a nation which was suffering from the culture shock of commercial growth.[23]   A final viewpoint in this category finds the ethical requirements of the prophets rooted in the *ethics of*

Kulttradition Israels in der Verkündigung des Propheten Micha (FRLANT 54; Göttingen: Vandenhoeck & Ruprecht, 1959) 42-64; R. Bergren, *The Prophets and the Law* (Cincinnati: Hebrew Union Press, 1974).

[21]   A. Alt, "Der Anteil des Konigtum an der sozialen Entwicklung in den Reichen Israel und Juda," *Kl Schr* III, 348-72; H. Donner, "Die soziale Botschaft der Propheten im Lichte der Gesellschaftsordnung," *Or Ant* 2 (1963) 229-45; G. Wanke, "Zu Grundlagen und Absicht prophetischer Sozialkritik," *KD* 18 (1972) 2-17; W. Dietrich, *Israel und Kanaan* (SBS 94; Stuttgart: Katholisches Bibelwerk, 1979). At times there is considerable overlap between the approach taken by these scholars and those of the previous category.

[22]   M. Weber, *Ancient Judaism* (Glencoe: The Free Press, 1952) 281; E. Troeltsch, "Glaube und Ethos der hebräischen Propheten," *Aufsätze zur Geistesgeschichte und Religionssoziologie* (Gesammelte Schriften 4; Tübingen: J. C. B. Mohr, 1925) 34-65. A. Causse, who followed these two scholars in a sociological approach, disagreed with the term utopian and suggested the prophets were concerned with "mystical values;" see his *Du Groupe ethnique à la communauté religieuse* (Paris: Felix Alcan, 1937) 92.

[23]   S. Nystrom, *Beduinentum und Jahwismus* (Lund: C. W. K. Gleerup, 1946) 123-26. His bibliography lists other scholars who support this view.

Canaanite society. The description of the king in the Ugaritic legends who "decided the case of the widow (and) judged the suit of the fatherless," was a cultural antecedent whose ethical presuppositions were mediated to and proclaimed by the prophetic figures in later Israel.[24]

(4) A fourth approach sees in the preaching of some prophets a basis in a *clan* or *tribal wisdom (Sippenethos)*. This interpretation stresses the similarity between the terminology and perspectives employed by the prophets and certain themes in wisdom literature. The similarity is then explained as a common background in a clan or village society which clashed with the goals of a state with more syncretistic and centralizing tendencies.[25]

(5) A fifth approach employs elements of *Marxist interpretation* in a study of the social conditions of Israelite society and the prophetic social critique. The prophets are perceived as representing *Urkommunismus* or protest against private property.[26] Many scholars who are not Marxist in their analysis nevertheless make pejorative references to capitalism and assert that eighth-century Israel had

---

[24]   E. Hammershaimb, "On the Ethics of the OT Prophets," *VTSup* 7 (1960) 75-101. According to O. Kaiser, "Gerechtigkeit und Heil," *NZSyTh* 11 (1969) 321, the prophets took their views on righteousness and salvation from nomadic ideals mixed with Canaanite ideals such as those reflected in the legend of King Keret.

[25]   H. W. Wolff, *Amos' geistige Heimat* (WMANT 18; Neukirchen-Vluyn: Neukirchener Verlag, 1964); E. Gerstenberger, *Wesen und Herkunft des "Apodiktischen Rechts"* (WMANT 20; Neukirchen-Vluyn: Neukirchener Verlag, 1965) 107, note 5; J. W. Whedbee, *Isaiah & Wisdom* (Nashville: Abingdon Press, 1971).

[26]   S. Holm-Nielsen, "Die Sozialkritik der Propheten," *Denkender Glaube* (ed. O. Kaiser; Berlin: de Gruyter, 1976) 8, and note 1, attributes to Ernst Bloch an influential role in viewing the prophets in a Marxist light, especially in his influence on modern German theology. See also, M. Lurje, *Studien zur Geschichte der wirtschaftlichen und sozialen Verhältnisse im israelitisch-judischen Reiche* (BZAW 45; Giessen: A Topelmann, 1927); J. Miranda, *Marx and the Bible* (Maryknoll: Orbis Books, 1974); N. Gottwald, *The Tribes of Yahweh* (Maryknoll: Orbis Books, 1979).

developed into a capitalistic society.[27]   A recent increase in the
tendency to view the eighth-century prophets as revolutionary and a
product of class conflict has been conjectured by Oswald Loretz.[28]

It should be stressed again that these are only representative
approaches. Most scholars, including those cited in the notes, are
dependent upon elements from several of these general positions.
Furthermore, each approach has its own strengths and weaknesses.
With regard to the first approach, it has been pointed out that an
emphasis on the moral character of God and prophetic individualism is
symptomatic of nineteenth-century ethical idealism, making the
prophets romantic figures while ignoring the specific location of the
prophetic ministry.[29]   Indeed this criticism is particularly important in
the segment of social criticism dealing with property rights, where
knowledge of the social setting and structure is invaluable. The fact
that many works present the historical and cultural background to the
prophetic social critique in such broad and abstract terms is unfortunate.
This shortcoming, however, provides an occasion for the present study
which is especially concerned with such a background.

The emphasis on the prophets as interpreters of the divine law
results partially from a reaction against an excessively negative view of
the law, an emphasis on the covenant as a basis for ethics, and from a
perceived similarity between the concerns of pentateuchal legislation

---

[27]   H. J. Kraus, "Die Prophetische Botschaft gegen das soziale
Unrecht Israel," *E v T* 15 (1955) 298; O. H. Steck, "Die
Gesellsschaftskritik der Propheten," *Christentum und Gesellschaft* (ed. B.
Lohse *et al.*; Göttingen: Vandenhoeck & Ruprecht, 1969) 53; H. W.
Wolff, *Amos and Joel* (Hermeneia; Philadelphia: Fortress Press, 1977)
69; R. B. Y. Scott, *The Relevance of the Prophets* (New York:
Macmillan, 1944) 30; J. L. Mays, *Micah* (OTL; Philadelphia:
Westminster, 1976) 71; Nystrom, *Beduinentum,* 128-29, 216; O. Kaiser,
"Gerechtigkeit," 313; Donner, "Botschaft," 238; Wanke, "Grundlagen,"
13. This is an abbreviated list.

[28]   O. Loretz, "Die prophetische Kritik des Rentenkapitalismus,"
UF 7 (1975) 272.   Evidently he is in agreement with Holm-Nielsen,
supra, note 26, that the tendency to view the prophets as examples of
class warfare has Marxist and anti-capitalistic overtones.

[29]   This is Troeltsch's criticism, "Glaube," 39-42, 50-51.

and the social views of the prophets.[30] As will be demonstrated in the first chapter (cf. Chart One), a high percentage of the parallels proposed between the prophets and the law do in fact concern property. These parallels, however, do not confirm this approach as a comprehensive explanation for the prophetic protest. The parallels are often of a general nature and there is not one uncontestable quotation of a legal text or statute in the eighth-century prophets.

In the third approach, the ideal of a *Gottesvolk* with the corresponding Israelite values of inalienable family property in the early postsettlement period raises several questions. An emphasis on Israel as the chosen people of YHWH is undeniable in the prophetic literature (Amos 3:2; Hos 11:1; Isa 5:1-7; Mic 3:5), as in the use of this motif in accusations. On the other hand, positing a "golden age" in the earliest period of Israel's settled history--an era very difficult for historians to reconstruct--is suspicious.[31] Moreover, the concept of inalienable property and especially the stress by many scholars on the corrupting influence of the Canaanites under the Israelite monarchy need to be reconsidered as our subsequent investigation will demonstrate.

The same may be said about other tendencies in this category. To describe the prophet's social exhortations as utopian does not adequately answer the question of source or authority and seems to confuse effect with intention. Concern for the widow and poor finds expression throughout the ancient Near East so that assuming the Israelites appropriated this concern from the Canaanites (known from the Ugaritic literature!) is unlikely.[32] In dealing with the more restricted question of property rights, the important question is the circumstances that gave rise to a concern for underprivileged segments of society.

The fourth approach suffers from the problem of a lack of criteria for determining what is distinctively wisdom literature and

---

[30]   As a sociologist and legal historian, Weber (*Judaism*, 61-89) did not deprecate the laws in the Pentateuch as did many of his Protestant contemporaries. He pointed out the essential congruence between some prophetic social demands and several legal stipulations.

[31]   This statement applies to such theories as the tribal league of M. Noth, *Das System der zwölf Stämme Israels* (BWANT 52; Leipzig: J. C. Hinrichs, 1930), or that of an ideal tribal nomadism as reconstructed by Nystrom, *Beduinentum*, and others.

[32]   F. C. Fensham, "Widow, Orphan and the Poor in Ancient Near Eastern Legal and Wisdom Literature," *JNES* 21 (1962) 129-30.

vocabulary[33] or, more specifically, the sources for Israelite clan wisdom.[34] This approach opposes an overemphasis on a revealed law as the basis for the prophetic protest and would link it instead to clan values. The strength of this approach is the presupposition that the clan and its ethos influenced the prophets' preaching; a view with some merit when one considers the importance of this socio-economic institution in Israelite society.[35] It must be concluded, however, that one cannot lump the effects of a clan/village ethos under the heading of "wisdom."

The fifth approach is important because it emphasizes socio-economic issues in the study of the prophetic social critique. Such an approach is necessary in the study of property rights. Marxist analysis, however, is finally inadequate and misleading with regard to prophecy and social criticism.[36] One reason is the irreducible theological character of prophecy itself. A more substantial reason is the ideological straitjacket with which many Marxists approach the ancient texts. For example, despite the many fine insights of Norman Gottwald's massive work,*The Tribes of Yahweh*, his description of early Israel as "classless"[37] is an anachronistic overstatement and an

---

[33]   J. L. Crenshaw, "The Influence of the Wise Upon Amos," *ZAW* 79 (1967) 42-51.

[34]   The Wisdom Literature of the Hebrew Bible does not always view the poor in a positive light, see A. Kuschke, "Arm und reich im Alten Testament mit besonder Berucksichtigung der nachexilischen Zeit," *ZAW* 59 (1939) 44-57.

[35]   Causse, *Groupe ethnique*, 15-94. Recent scholarship has returned to an interest in the influence of the tribal/clan and village social structure in ancient Israel, see Gottwald, *Tribes of Yahweh*; and F. Crüsemann, *Der Widerstand gegen das Königtum* (WMANT 49; Neukirchen-Vluyn: Neukirchener Verlag, 1978), esp.   194-222. Crüsemann analyses Israel's tribal system using sociological and anthropological material.

[36]   This rejection of Marxist (and capitalistic) ideology as the determining factor in investigating ancient societies follows the views of K. Polanyi, *Trade and Market in the Early Empires: Economies in History and Theory* (Chicago: The Free Press, 1957); M. Nash, *Primitive and Peasant Economic Systems* (San Francisco: Chandler, 1966); T. F. Carney, *The Economies of Antiquity* (Lawrence: Coronado Press, 1973).

[37]   Gottwald, *Tribes*, 700.   More frequently he uses the term "egalitarian," which Crüsemann (*Der Widerstand*, 206) rejects as

attempt to provide a biblical basis for his own deeply held views. The prophets become for him "the logical development" from this foundational period. In reality this view is another example of the "golden age" theory where an ideal is reconstructed for an earlier phase of existence. A second example comes from J. Miranda's work, *Marx and the Bible*, where he states that Jeremiah was aware of and opposed the dangers of private property[38] --on the assumption that the prophets were proto-Marxists--while overlooking the statement of the prophet in YHWH's name that, "houses and fields and vineyards shall again be bought in this land (Jer 32:15)." Perhaps the fundamental reason why Marxist ideology, and capitalistic ideology as well, are inadequate is that both bring anachronistic assumptions to bear on a non-western, pre-industrial society. In pre-exilic Israel there is little evidence of a large private market (either to advocate or criticize), a large pool of surplus laborers, or a widespread monetization of relationships. Marxist scholars have stressed the importance of private ownership as a cause of class tensions, but the issue of private property or ownership is misleading for understanding pre-exilic Israel; in some cases the "proletariat" possessed the means of production yet were still perceived as oppressed.

Before concluding this survey, there are a few scholars whose work is closely related to the subject of property rights in the prophetic literature and who thus deserve more than a brief reference (all but the first scholar have been mentioned in the above survey). Issues and concepts dealt with in their work are important for the present topic.

Franz Walter[39]

Walter was not a biblical scholar yet he attempted to place the prophets within "Jewish economic history." He was a product of the late nineteenth century and accepted the results of recent scholarship that posited a development in Israel from a primitive to a commercial society by the eighth century. Solomon's excesses as king played a crucial role in Walter's understanding. His building projects and

---

unsociological including the specific term "classless." See the reviews of Gottwald by M. J. Buss and G. Lenski in *RStR* 6 (1980) 271-78.

[38]   Miranda, *Marx*, 20.

[39]   F. Walter, *Die Propheten in ihrem sozialen Beruf und das Wirtschaftsleben ihrer Zeit* (Freiburg: Breisgau, 1900).

commercial endeavors along with capitalism, that driving tendency for development, were primarily responsible for the sad economic conditions in later years. Both the eighth-century prophets and the "Mosaic" law expressed care for the poor and opposed the effects of capitalism. While it is true, he concluded, that the reforming views of the prophets were utopian and similar to communism, they were also patriots whose main point was clear: "Rückkehr zur Agrarpolitik und Erhaltung des bäuerlichen Mittelstandes."[40]

Walter's work has been relegated to obscurity because it was considered merely an attempt by an ethicist to speak to the German states in 1900. On the other hand, it is a good summary of then current opinion and did point out several issues such as the role of kingship and capitalism that remain the concerns of scholars. While his pronouncements on utopianism and communism fall wide of the mark, his almost intuitive insight that agrarian relations in Israel were deteriorating by the eighth century remains a view of some substance.

Albrecht Alt

Alt's essay on social development under the monarchy[41] has been the single most influential work from a socio-economic perspective in the study of prophecy and social criticism, especially among German speaking scholars. This is true in spite of the fact that he did not treat many of the prophetic texts themselves in any detail. His point of departure was the conditions pertaining to Israel in the early settlement period. Micah 2:2b, "A man and his house, a man and his inheritance (naḥalāh)," was for Alt a succinct statement of the economic ideal in early Israel. The land was seen as YHWH's possession with the Israelite farmer or herdsman his usufructuary. For this reason one's family heritage was inalienable. Settlement in Palestine and the rise of the Israelite monarchy meant the incorporation of indigenous peoples (i.e., the Canaanites) into a newly formed state. Because the Canaanites had lived for centuries in socially stratified city-states, some of their administrative personnel now served the new state. The chariot corps of the former city-states were adopted by David and his successors along with taxation and conscription measures. Most important were the new property rights of the royal house and of these Canaanite citizens in

---

40   *Ibid.*, 259-60.
41   *Supra.*, note 21. See also Chapter Two, *infra.*

Israel. Members of the former acquired extensive holdings through conquest, purchase and appropriation, and granted portions of their estate to loyal servants. The latter viewed property, according to Alt, as another form of capital and encouraged the free alienation of land. Thus there were two contrasting types of *Bodenrecht* at work in society with the new rights and demands of the king as an added factor. Both the practices of free alienation of land and royal land grants were more conducive to commerce than the earlier Israelite ideal so that they tended to replace the previous Yahwistic practices. Alt did not examine the prophetical texts in any detail but he did point out that most accusations concerning property rights are made against officials and the upper classes and not against the king.

Alt's reconstruction plays a prominent role in the discussion of prophecy and social criticism in the works of such scholars as Kraus,[42] Donner,[43] Wanke,[44] von Rad,[45] Fohrer,[46] Wolff,[47] and Herrmann.[48] While some aspects of his reconstruction are persuasive, there are two conclusions that deserve examination and either modification or rejection. The first is his concept of inalienable property, which requires at least some additional effort at clarification. The second is his assessment of Canaanite influence in general and the particular assertion of the replacement of Israelite practices by Canaanite customs. Donner, who follows Alt very closely, has taken an even more extreme position with regard to the Canaanite influence on property rights:

> Die Bescheltungen der Propheten richten sich ausschliesslich (!) gegen die kanaanaische oder kanaanisierte Oberschicht und

---

[42]   *Supra.*, note 27.

[43]   *Supra.*, note 21.

[44]   *Supra.*, note 21.

[45]   *Supra.*, note 16. Von Rad opines (p. 23, note 35) that Israel and Judah adopted the laws of Canaan in the economic sphere.

[46]   G. Fohrer, "Zur Einwirkung der gesellschaftlichen Struktur Israels auf seine Religion," *Near Eastern Studies in honor of William Foxwell Albright* (ed. H. Goedicke; Baltimore: Johns Hopkins, 1971) 181.

[47]   Wolff, *Amos*, 194 and his footnote 28.

[48]   S. Herrmann, *A History of Israel in Old Testament Times* (Philadelphia: Fortress Press, 1975) 235-40.

Beamtenschaft, gegen ihre Eingriffe in die alten Ordnung des Rechtslebens und der Grundbesitzverhältnisse.[49]

This statement by Donner is prompted by Alt's work and is reflected in a somewhat less dogmatic form in the works of the scholars noted above.

Klaus Koch

Koch's work[50] contains a valuable survey of previous opinions on the subject of prophecy and social criticism as well as substantial insights of his own. His research on the socio-economic background to this criticism leads him to posit a class of *Kleinbauern* in northern Israel who are losing their property and citizenship rights. Taxation, lending with interest, and the perversion of local administration by powerful persons are the primary measures opposed by Amos. Koch makes an important observation with regard to the administration of justice in local communities, and the conflict over the property rights of those who collect taxes (in kind) as opposed to the taxed, the creditor as opposed to the debtor, and the slaveowner as opposed to his human property:

Der Schlussakt, der Eintritt eines bislang freien Kleinbauern in die Schuldsklaverei wird in vielen Fallen gar keinen Spruch der Ortsgemeinde erfordert haben, zumal die Gläubiger, die Amos angreift, nicht in den Dörfern sondern in den Hauptstädten sitzen und vermutlich die Torgemeinde gar nicht als Gerichtsort anerkannt hätten."[51]

The importance of Koch's statement lies in his recognition of the fact, also noted by others,[52] that the local administrative/judicial system was perceived as not adequately protecting the property rights of certain people, and perhaps was helpless because of the power of the creditors. Whether these oppressed people are best described as "small farmers" may be overlooked for the present as may his conclusions concerning

---

49   Donner, "Botschaft," 243-44.
50   *Supra., note* 17.
51   *Ibid.,* 246.
52   E. g., Donner, "Botschaft," 236-38; Weber, *Judaism,* 19-20.

the silence of the local system of administration over entrance into debt slavery. Evidently some local administrative institutions were not functioning to safeguard citizens' rights. The whole question of the relationship between local (and more centralized) administrative/judicial systems and the exercise of property rights requires a thorough investigation (see Chapter Three).

Oswald Loretz[53]

This scholar states that the work of Alt and "his school" has set the investigation of the prophetic protests on the right track. His own contribution is the suggestion that the geographer H. Bobek's theory of *Rentenkapitalismus* best describes the economic system opposed by the prophets. *Rentenkapitalismus*[54] is a system that develops out of an agrarian society but precedes a productive, industrial capitalism. It is characteristic of an oriental civilization with a developing urban and commercial base (there are modern examples), and differs from modern capitalism because it "nicht mit Production verbindet, sondern sich mit dem Abschöpfen ihrer Erträge begnügt."[55]

Loretz argues that this system is generally a characteristic of the ancient Near East and that the prophets were not unique in opposing its development in Israel. He provides few specific examples or references to ancient literature and seems content to quote Bobek. His reconstruction is important in again raising the issue of pre-exilic Israel's social and economic structure, and in attempting an identification of that structure with *Rentenkapitalismus*. The term is unfortunate, however, because of its modern connotations; even though Loretz notes the differences with modern capitalism, his assertion of its near ubiquity in the ancient Near East makes the term of little real value in analyzing the specifics of the prophetic protests. Furthermore, his contrast of this socio-economic system with that of a *nomadischen Lebenswelt* which nurtured the prophets is not convincing at all.

---

53   *Supra.*, note 28.
54   *Ibid.*, 274-75 and footnotes 31-37 for references to Bobek's works.
55   *Ibid.*, 276.

Enough has been written, however briefly, to provide an overview of scholarly opinion.[56]   The references and categories were chosen in view of their relevance to the more restricted topic of the dissertation. There are several other facets of prophecy and social criticism (*e.g.*, criticism of the cult, luxury, drunkenness, hubris, *etc.*) which would deserve treatment in any extended survey.

The Present Study

The present study will begin, in the first chapter, with an investigation of the prophetical literature. The task is to collect and exegete all of the references to property rights in the literature that can reasonably be dated to the designated time period of the eighth century. As stated previously, many of the references are found in passages which form-critics have termed "accusations" or "reproaches," so that to some extent the study is involved in reconstructing a perceived social conflict. The investigation will attempt to answer two basic questions: (1) what are the fundamental or primary rights referred to or assumed when property is mentioned, and (2) who is responsible, if anyone, for their violation or administration?   This first chapter will provide preliminary answers to both questions and set the stage for the following chapters.

The second chapter will concentrate on the rights to possess and alienate immovable property (land, houses), because these rights are obviously an issue with the eighth-century prophets. Conclusions drawn from this chapter will provide a negative judgment on the widespread assertion that Canaanite customs had replaced Israelite practices in the realm of land tenure rights, and support for the view, derived from the results of the first chapter, that various state and local officials play a large role in the perceived conflict.

The third chapter will begin with an investigation of the Israelite administrative/judicial system, especially regarding its relationship to

---

56   At least three other works deserve a reference: M. Fendler, "Zur Sozialkritik des Amos," *EvT* 33 (1973) 32-53; M. A. Cohen, "The Prophets as Revolutionaries: A Socio-Political Analysis," *BAR* 5 (1979) 12-19; M. J. Buss, "The Social Psychology of Prophecy," *Prophecy. Essays presented to Georg Fohrer* (BZAW 150; Berlin: de Gruyter, 1980) 1-11.   Buss points out that ecstatic religion--a component of the prophetic faith--serves as a vehicle for protest against stratification in society.

the exercise of property rights. The prophets themselves record a negative view of this relationship and the conclusion will be drawn that a state bureaucracy and administrative/judicial system that developed under the monarchy often overlay the more traditional local system of administration and was a source of conflict.

The fourth chapter is an investigation of the property rights and privileges accorded state officials concluding that these rights (*e.g.*, taxation and possession of land grants) could easily lead to friction with the rights of other citizens. The results from this chapter will be correlated with those from previous chapters to provide additional support for conclusions reached earlier.

A fifth chapter will assess the conclusions from the previous four and attempt a partial answer to the question: why the perceived conflict in the eighth century? The chapter will conclude that the typical and widespread answer of rapid commercial development is one important factor but that external historical factors such as the influence of the Neo-Assyrian empire also played an important role.

The questions asked and the approach taken in this study are primarily socio-economic and historical in nature. This is because, as Siegfried Herrmann[57]   has recently observed, the best method of approaching the perceived social conflict of the eighth century is a study of the socio-economic conditions of the period. Indeed, as Herrmann also observed, there is a need for studies in this area and of this particular nature. This means that the influential views of Alt and those who generally follow his reconstruction will receive extended treatment because their suggestions take socio-economic structure and the immediate historical context into account.

---

[57]   Herrmann, *A History*, 237.

Chapter One

The Eighth Century Prophets

Amos

The following passages in the book of Amos are relevant to the present study: 2:6b-8, 3:9-10, 5:11a, and 7:1b. All but the last text contain accusations against the misuse of property. The last text, while not an accusation, is a reference to the right of the king to collect a tax or payment in kind.

The book of Amos begins with a series of prophecies directed against eight Syro-Palestinian states,[1] with the last and longest prophecy addressing Israel. These prophecies have certain common characteristics as form-critics have emphasized:[2] common to all being (1) an introduction as the speech of YHWH and (2) a graduated numerical saying accompanied by examples of crimes. The fundamental point is that the future judgment announced by YHWH is inseparably related to the present enumeration of crimes, acts which in themselves illustrate a violated moral order.

The prophecy against Israel (2:6-16), Amos's original audience, contains an expansion of the second characteristic. It contains a brief historical resume in which Amos[3] includes not only the traditions about the exodus and conquest, but also of YHWH's provisions for settled existence with his reference to the institutions of prophecy and the Nazirites (2:11-12).[4] The reference to the granting of the land is important, for Amos's accusations have their basis in the misuse of the gifts of land and settled existence.

---

[1]   For the discussion concerning the authenticity of these prophecies, see H. W. Wolff, *Joel and Amos* (Philadelphia: Fortress Press, 1977) 135-42; W. Rudolph, *Joel-Amos-Obadja-Jona* (KAT 13/2; Gütersloh: Gerd Mohn, 1971) 118-124.

[2]   D. Christensen, *Transformations of the War Oracle in Old Testament Prophecy* (HDR 3; Missoula: Scholars Press, 1975) 55-72.

[3]   Rudolph (*Amos*, 145-46) has persuasively argued that 2:9-11 is integral to the prophet's argument.

[4]   The mention of prophecy and Nazirites in the summary of *Heilsgeschichte* is only here among the summaries in the Hebrew Bible.

Amos 2:6b-8[5]

Because of those who sell the righteous for money
And the poor for a pair of sandals;
Who trample the head of the poor (upon the dust of the earth),
And pervert the way of the afflicted *(ʿanāwīm)*
For a man and his father go into a maiden,
In order to profane my holy name.
Upon pledged garments they spread out beside every altar,
And wine taken in exaction they drink in the house of their God.

In this passage, the prophet does not specifically name those responsible for these crimes(pešaʿīm, 2:6a), thus one must work from internal evidence in determining the nature and, if possible, the perpetrators of these deeds. The term for crime, *pšʿ*, has several related meanings, but Wolff has persuasively shown that in Amos the word refers to cases that "exclusively involve infractions of property and personal rights," citing context and the occurrence of the word in the legal traditions (Exod 22:8) as evidence.[6]

There is almost universal agreement in understanding the reference to "selling people" as denoting debt slavery, an institution presupposed and regulated in Israel's legal traditions and referred to in the narrative sections of the Hebrew Bible as well.[7] In the ancient Near East, people and their property were exchanged to fulfill obligations or in place of the fulfillment of obligations. The chief reason for slavery was probably indebtedness.[8] Elsewhere, Amos uses similar terminology, although using the verb *qnh* instead of *mkr*, as a reference to the way people were forced into debt slavery (8:6). In this latter reference, the quotation placed in the mouth of the creditor makes it clear that he can buy or acquire a debtor.

---

[5]   In addition to the commentaries see, M. A. Beek, "The Religious Background of Amos 2:6-8," *OTS* 5 (1948) 132-41.

[6]   Wolff (*Amos*, 152-53). This view opposes the interpretation of the oracles against foreign nations as a response to a violation of the "Davidic League," as argued by Christensen (*Transformations*, 55-72).

[7]   Exod 21:1-11; Lev 25:39; Deut 15:12; 2 Kings 4:1-7; Neh 5:5.

[8]   So I. Mendelsohn, *Slavery in the Ancient Near East* (New York: Oxford University Press, 1949) 23.

The "righteous" are those perceived by Amos as innocent of any wrong-doing, probably in the legal sense of the word (Exod 23:7). This reference to legal innocence does not exhaust the meaning of the word; it has a further positive meaning derived from the cult and communal life as a characteristic term for "den freien Volks-und Kultgenossen, dessen gemeinschaftsgemässes Verhalten als selbstverständlich gilt und der deshalb unbeschränkt kultrechts-und wehrfähig ist."[9] The parallel with the "poor" does not mean the righteous are propertyless; in fact, the various references to the poor and oppressed in Amos presuppose that certain classes of citizens are losing their property,[10] even though they had been upright in their affairs.[11]

The possible juristic connotation of "righteous" suggests to some that in 2:6b corrupt judges and bribery are the perpetrators and the crime respectively.[12] Most recent scholars, however, see the accusation as a condemnation of a creditor.[13] This may be a false alternative, for the whole passage (2:6b-8) describes various features in a complex *process* in which the basic social institutions of Israelite society are seen as no longer upholding YHWH's moral order. Like Israel's neighbors and the Nazirites they have fallen prey to corruption so that they now stand as reasons for the coming judgment. Both interpretations, either corrupt judges or rapacious creditors, are illustrations of this perceived corruption.[14]

---

[9]   Koch, "Die Entstehung," 244.   He believes the traditional language from the Psalms concerning the righteous and the afflicted has influenced Amos.

[10]   Amos does not even mention widows and orphans, usually the most destitute of persons in antiquity.

[11]   They are righteous in the prophet's eye because they have not violated community standards yet they have become the property of others.   See Rudolph, *Amos*, 140-41; M. Schwantes, *Das Recht der Armen* (BET 4; Frankfurt: Peter Lang, 1977) 92, note 4.

[12]   E. Sellin, *Das Zwölfprophetenbuch*(KAT 12/1; Leipzig: A. Deitchert, 1929) 206-7; T. H. Robinson, *Die Zwölf Kleinen Propheten* (HAT 14; Tübingen: J. C. B. Mohr, 1954) 78-79.

[13]   Wolff, *Amos*, 165; Rudolph, *Amos*, 141; J. Mays, *Amos* (OTL; Philadelphia: Westminster Press, 1969) 45.

[14]   Perhaps those who judged were the creditors.   As will be demonstrated in Chapter Four, in other texts from the ancient Near East there is evidence that administrative officials also served as creditors.

The reference to a pair of sandals reflects what was probably an idiomatic phrase (cf. Amos 8:6; 1 Sam 12:3, LXX). The Greek text of the Samuel passage has the aged judge say, "from whose hand have I taken a bribe or a pair of shoes?"[15] A pair of shoes is not merely a trifling, especially not in parallel to money or a bribe, but a symbol of the exchange of property rights and a token of possession. Ruth 4:7-8 records the custom of the gift of a sandal as confirmation of the transaction between Boaz and the unnamed kinsman. The shoe as a symbol of possession is perhaps behind the phrase, "upon Edom I cast my shoe" (Ps 60:10). As such, this symbol has cultural parallels in the Nuzi texts and in the Middle Ages in Europe.[16] Evidently, a creditor's acquisition of a person included the "legal fiction" of a sandal exchange (or gift), with any communal opposition to the purchase being circumvented by portraying the act as a simple exchange of goods.

The addition of, ʿal ʿapar ʾereṣ, in 7a is probably evidence for the earliest interpretation of the previous verse concerning debt slavery, and one which exegetes have ingnored since recognizing the secondary character of the phrase. Translating hašoʾapīm "trample" assumes a participle derived from the rare word šûp, found in Gen 3:15.[17] It seems an early editor understood the crime correctly as an attempt to acquire property, particularly land, as well as the person of the debtor, but read the verb incorrectly as a derivative of šʾp, "to yearn" or "long

---

[15]   The Greek text and a discussion can be found in G. H. Box, "Amos 2:6 and 8:6," *Exp Tim* 12 (1900-01) 377-78. R Gordis, "Studies in the Book of Amos," *American Academy for Jewish Research* 46-47 (1979-80) 213-15, has argued that the word translated "sandal," naʿalayim, should be derived from the root ʿlm, meaning "to conceal" or "bribe." While his arguments make some sense for 2:6, bribery does not fit the context of 8:6.

[16]   E. R. Lachmann, "Note on Ruth 4:7-8," *JBL* 56 (1939) 53-56; E. A. Speiser, "Of Shoes and Shekels," *BASOR* 77 (1940) 15-20. Speiser discusses the custom found in the Nuzi texts where such items as shoes and cloaks "were regarded as token payments to validate special transactions by lending them the appearance of normal business practice" (p. 17). In the Middle Ages a glove symbolized a transaction in certain areas of Europe; W. Gesenius, *Hebrew and Chaldee Lexicon* (Grand Rapids: Eerdmans, 1949) 554.

[17]   Wolff, *Amos*, 133k; Gordis ("Amos," 212) calls the participle in 2:7a "a metaplastic form for the *mediae Vav suph*."

for."[18] The result was the MT and an understanding of the acquisition of debtors as a yearning for all the property of the poor, including even the dust of his land found on his body.[19]

Evidence for the failure of Israel's social institutions to administer YHWH's will is found in the phrase, "they turn aside the way of the afflicted." The same verb, *nth* is also used by Amos in describing the perversion of the legal process in the gate of a village (5:12), a process and social setting that are probably referred to in 2:7 as well.[20] It is likely that local, commercial transactions concerning property were conducted in the gate of the appropriate town, especially where citizens of the town would be affected (Ruth 4:1-12; Gen 23:3-16, esp. v 10). Where judges and elders were present, either to witness and confirm or to adjudicate, the possibility of corruption was present too. This possibility is especially true in terms of conflict of interests whereby the local citizens (officials) who conducted the gate proceedings might receive material benefit from the economic misfortunes of a neighbor. The local administration of justice was, ideally speaking, to be a leveling mechanism where citizens could have some control over their own affairs, but this is not the function portrayed in 2:7a.

Copulation with the same female by a man and his father profanes YHWH's name (2:7b). Unfortunately, the female or maiden *(na'arāh)* is not further identified, leading some to the conclusion that the act is a violation of the laws of consanguinity.[21] Casuistic law in the Book of the Covenant provides for certain rights of a female slave *('āmāh)* including the implication that she should not be forced to become the concubine for both father and son (Exod 21:7-11). In the particular case of Exod 21:7-11, the female bondservant was sold by her father into

---

18   Beek, "Background," 135.

19   Several older commentators saw in the mention of dust a reference to the poor man's land; see W. R. Harper, *Amos and Hosea* (ICC; New York: Charles Scribner's Sons, 1905) 49-50.

20   The verb *nth* occurs several times in references to the perverting of the administrative/judicial process. Cf. 1 Sam 8:3; Amos 5:12; Exod 23:2, 6; Isa 10:2, 29:21, 30:11; Deut 16:19.

21   So Wolff (*Amos*, 167) pointing to Lev 18:15, 20:12. The suggestion that the woman is actually a temple prostitute is not confirmed by other uses of the word *na'arāh* see *infra*, note 23.

slavery and is considered the property of her owner.[22] As a possible concubine or daughter-in-law, she also has certain rights. This reference in Amos probably reflects a similar situation where a maiden has been sold or relinquished to a creditor and has lost even the rights of a legal concubine. The word na‘arāh can mean servant,[23] yet it is the immediate context of debt slavery and oppression which argues for as much concern on the part of the prophet for the maiden and her rights as for the violation of the laws of consanguinity.

Pledges for security on loans and exactions in kind conclude the list of crimes. Various objects were forbidden or strictly regulated as employment for security according to the legal traditions because they were essential to life and commerce (Deut 24:6, 12-13, 17; Exod 22:25). A garment or overcoat was one of these objects. Spreading out garments taken in pledge--almost certainly showing intent to keep them overnight--violates such ordinances.[24] There is also the possibility that the use of these pledged garments in a temple would have sanctified them and thus forbidden their removal. The point, then, would be that a greedy creditor would use a pledged garment for a cultic observance rather than "dedicate" or lose one of his own.[25]

Payment of obligations in kind, especially with set measures of liquid commodities, is common in an agricultural setting (2 Kings 4:1-

---

[22]   Mendelsohn (*Slavery*, 13) writes that Exod 21:7-11 probably represents "a fragment of a series of enactments that originally dealt with all cases of conditional sales of young girls." We are suggesting that Amos opposes the violation of the rights of protection of young girls who are the objects of "conditional sales." The father and son are exercising "property rights" that they, according to Amos, should not have.

[23]   Against R. Bach, "Gottesrecht," 30-31. See the list of references compiled by V. Maag, *Text, Wortschatz und Begriffswelt des Buches Amos* (Leiden: E. J. Brill, 1951) 177, note 9.

[24]   Cf. Mic 2:8b and Excursus One in Chapter Three.

[25]   J. Morgenstern, "Amos Studies (Part Four)," *HUCA* 32 (1961) 316. He uses the reference to a wardrobe in 2 Kings 10:22 as evidence that a special garment would be required for participants at a shrine. His emendation of *yaṭṭû* to *ya‘aṭû* "they put on," is neither necessary nor convincing.

7).[26] Israel's legal traditions recognize compensation measures to be taken in certain cases (cf. Exod 21:22; Deut 22:19), where the same term ʿānāš is used. It is not clear whether the wine is compensation for damages, though this is unlikely, or perhaps a payment (interest?) on a debt; nor why the consumption of the wine is held to be a crime.[27] The word ʿōnāš is used for a forced exaction (tribute) in 2 Kings 23:33 so that the reference to wine from those "fined" *(RSV)* in 2:8 probably does not refer to compensation at all but to a forced exaction such as a payment, or most likely some form of tax.[28] Perhaps the deleterious effect of wine on those responsible for protecting the rights of the poor is also in view in this reference (cf. Isa 5:22-23). In any case, one should recognize that the rights of those who had been the subject of exaction are the concern of the prophet as well as the indictment of the person(s) who consumed the beverage.

Amos 2:6b-8 sketches briefly, by citing examples, the process of perceived social and economic ruination which engulfed the "righteous." Each crime involved the loss or misuse of property, whether it concerned the entrance of people into debt slavery or the forfeiture of possessions. The only exception to this is possibly 2:7b, but in that case it is more likely that the "rights" of the maiden are being violated as well. Closely related to this conclusion is the denial and/or perversion of "due process" as recorded in 2:7ab.

---

26   Wolff, *Amos*, 168, (incorrectly) thinks of money used to purchase wine. For alcoholic beverages as a medium of exchange see, M. Nash, *Primitive and Peasant Economic Systems*, 76-77.

27   Perhaps the crime is related to the location in a temple, although Amos does not seem concerned elsewhere for the sanctity of a temple! Wolff (*Amos*, 134) has even argued that the references to an altar and temple in v 8ab and bb are secondary (editorial). Compensation payments were to go to the injured party so that the reference is probably not to priests either.

28   See 1 Kings 10:15 where the Greek (LXX) and Targum seem to presuppose a reading ʿōnešē "exactions," for MT which has ʾanšē, "men." The verse is a description of Solomon's sources of wealth so that the reference to exactions of (from) the merchants as the Greek has it is probably original. Later tariff inscriptions use the cognate noun ʿnšm to mean a tax; R. S. Tomback, *A Comparative Semitic Lexicon of the Phoenician and Punic Languages* (SBLDS 32; Missoula: Scholars Press, 1978) 253.

Finally, Wolff's statement, "it is not possible to conclude from the tone of Amos' accusation that he rejected slavery for debt as a legal institution altogether," is misleading.[29] Nowhere does Amos' recorded prophecy contain any positive statement concerning slavery and this applies both to the statements against the Philistines (1:6) and Tyre (1:9) as well as Israel. In another context, Exod 21:37 mandates slavery for a cattle thief who is apprehended but cannot make restitution, in essence a form of debt slavery. It is quite possible that such a measure would have been deemed appropriate by Amos, which suggests Wolff ultimately is correct. But that is speculation. The only evidence remaining in the book of Amos records not reform but condemnation of the effects of this institution.[30]

Amos 3:9-10

Proclaim upon the strongholds of Ashdod,
And upon the strongholds in the land of Egypt;
(and say), 'Collect yourselves on the mountains of Samaria,
And see the great tumults in her midst,
And the oppression within her.
They do not know how to do the right thing--YHWH's word--
Those who store up violence and devastation in their strongholds.'

The whole passage, including the conclusion of v 11, demonstrates how clearly the prophet depicts the relationship between corrupt economic

---

[29]   Wolff, *Amos*, 165.

[30]   Bach ("Gottesrecht" 29) believes Amos opposed debt slavery because it was regulated by casuistic law (according to him, of Canaanite origin and profane) but went against the principles of apodictic or genuinely Israelite law. His understanding of casuistic law and its origin is dependent upon A. Alt, "The Origins of Israelite Law," *Old Testament History and Religion* (Garden City: Doubleday & Co., 1966) 103-71. That only apodictic law was genuinely Israelite, as held by Alt, Bach and others, has been shown false; see R. Kilian, "Apodiktisches und kasuistische Recht im Licht agyptischer Analogien," *BZ* 7 (1963) 185-202, and S. Gevirtz, "West-Semitic Curses and the Problem of the Origins of Hebrew Law," *VT* 11 (1961) 137-58. Amos did oppose various cases (typical examples?) of economic oppression which may have some support in casuistic-formulated laws, but his opposition does not seem predicated on their Canaanite background.

circumstances and the coming future disaster. This relationship is highlighted by the results of form-critical investigation: Two witnesses are called to see the situation and hear YHWH's pronouncement for the future. The summons to Ashdod and Egypt is not coincidental; as two former oppressors of Israel (Ashdod=Philistines) they are called as witnesses (Deut 19:15) to see the capital city of Samaria now playing a similar role of oppression.[31] Originally a call to proclaim *may* have had its life setting in the commissioning of emissaries[32] but now it functions in the present context as the first part of an indictment against Samaria for misappropriation of property and economic oppression. For a good view, the witnesses are to assemble on the hills surrounding Samaria in order to see the type of society which inhabits the summit.

The language of oppression employed by Amos in this text is general, almost stereotypical, so that little specific information can be derived from it.[33] The terminology does indicate, however, that the oppression is primarily economic and that the word pair, *ḥāmās wāšōd* signifies, "die an Gut und Besitz verübte Gewalt."[34] Wolff, as a typical example, concludes that rich and leading citizens of Samaria have stored up fortunes in their "houses" at the expense of the less fortunate. As a general conclusion this is undoubtedly correct, but it misses a distinction the passage makes regarding Samaria and its inhabitants. Specifically, the former oppressors are to assemble on the mountain*s* of Samaria so that they may see the disorder on the mountai*n* of Samaria (cf. 4:1, 6:1 where the singular is also used). The point is that the city built by Omri and Ahab was largely if not exclusively a royal administrative center on an acropolis. Additional public buildings and protective walls had been added by Amos' time but

---

[31]   For this reason the Ashdod of the MT is to be preferred against many commentators who read "Assyria" with the Greek.

[32]   Wolff, *Amos*, 119.

[33]   For example, Jer 6:1-8 refers to "strongholds, oppression, violence and devastation," using the same terminology as Amos 3:9-10, but the context is that of the calls to flee and to battle.

[34]   The quote is from I. L. Seeligmann, "Zur Terminologie fur das Gerichtsverfahren im Wortschatz des biblischen Hebraische," *Hebraische Wortforschung, VTSup* 16 (1974) 257. Some examples of the word *ʿšq*, "to oppress," where the reference is to economic oppression, are 1 Sam 12:3-4; Mic 2:2; Hos 12:8; Jer 21:12, 22:17; Ezek 22:7, 22:29; Prov 14: 31, 22:16.

the function of the summit remained the same throughout the pre-exilic period. The common people of Samaria evidently lived on the eastern slope of the hill where the present village of *Sebaste* is now located.[35] Thus, the call to see the disorder and oppression in Samaria referred to the hill of Samaria and to its residents on the summit who were (officially) responsible for the affairs of the state.

The catchword, ʾarmānôt, also supports the interpretation that mere private houses and the anonymous rich are *not* primarily in the prophet's mind. This word, meaning palace and/or stronghold,[36] is a national or royal possession elsewhere in the book of Amos (1:4,7,10,12,14, 2:2,5, 6:8). The reference to the strongholds of Ashdod and Egypt implies the same connotation in the present reference. Elsewhere, an ʾarmōn is associated with the royal palace (1 Kings 16:18; in Samaria, 2 Kings 15:25). It has walls (Lam 2:7) and is paralleled with a city (Isa 25:2, 32:14) or fortress (Isa 34:13). Perhaps the chiastic arrangement of Hos 8:14 is the best indication of definition: "Israel has forgotten his maker and built palaces *(hêkālôt)*, and Judah has multiplied fortified cities: but I will send fire on his cities and consume his strongholds *(ʾarmānôt, BHS)*."

The collecting of "oppression" in these strongholds does not just refer to houses--although it is probable that these ʾarmānôt were used for dwellings--but to those public buildings used also for storerooms which were located in Samaria throughout the pre-exilic period. These were buildings where property and goods originally acquired for *government* use and distribution would be stored.[37]

The oppression that Amos perceives, therefore, takes on a more definite focus even though many of the specific measures opposed are still obscure. Amos's repeated verbal attacks on Samaria, however, are a good indication of the ultimate source of conflict with regard to his other explicitly stated accusations (esp. 2:6b-8, 5:11). Evidently royal policy and influence were perceived as major contributors to the socio-economic problems associated with property rights.

---

[35]   J. W. Crowfoot, K. Kenyon, E. L. Sukenik, *The Buildings at Samaria* (Samaria-Sebaste I; London: Palestine Exploration Fund, 1942) 94-111. According to the present state of knowledge, "we are left with the impression that the capital was administrative only," K. Kenyon, *Royal Cities of the Old Testament* (London: Barric & Jenkins, 1971) 82.

[36]   *KB*, 86.

[37]   The Samaria Ostraca were found in a room of such a building.

Amos 5:11a

Because you place exactions[38] on the poor,
And take grain tribute from him.

This accusation is embedded in a larger passage (5:1-17) whose method of composition is disputed. One question concerns the accusation of 5:11a and its role: was it an independent piece or was it part of an original prophecy against those who hate an advocate of right in the gate (5:7,10)? The latter choice is more probable and as the text is now arranged, v 11a is an illustration of the situation that evoked a cry of "woe" in 5:1.[39]

Translators of the *hapax legomenon, bōšaskem*, have generally opted for one of two choices: (1) Deriving the word from *bûs* meaning to "trample,"[40] or (2) seeing a metathesis of consonants from a verb whose cognate is found in the common Akkadian idiom, *šabašu šibša ina eqli*, "to take rent from a field" (cf. note 38). Verse 11a makes it clear that exactions in kind are the issue and thus the second translation provides a synonymous parallelism. This second translation or view is adopted with caution in this study.[41]

The majority of scholars interpret the accusation of v 11a as a comment on the evils of tenant farming (a *metayage* system). The primary reference could be either to debtors who are paying off the interest on a loan by sharing the harvest of a crop or to the worker who farms someone else's land for a small percentage of the crop. Such a

---

38   Following *KB*, 158, "Getreidepacht erheben." So also Mays, *Amos*, 90; Wolff, *Amos*, 230; and M. Fendler, "Zur Sozialkritik des Amos,"*EvT* 33 (1973) 37. For complete philological details, *infra*, note 41.

39   J. De Waard, "The Chiastic Structure of Amos V 1-17," *VT* 27 (1977) 170-77. Mays is probably correct (*Amos*, 90) in reconstructing an original woe speech in 5:7, 10-11.

40   J. Wellhausen, *Die Kleinen Propheten* (Berlin: de Gruyter, 1963) 82.

41   H. R. Cohen, *Biblical Hapax Legomena in the Light of Akkadian and Ugaritic* (SBLDS 37; Missoula: Scholars Press, 1978) 49, concludes that this translation is "established." This judgment is too optimistic.

person would have to meet certain contractual obligations before receiving any benefit himself. Tenant farming does not have a clear reference elsewhere in the Hebrew Bible and was probably not a common practice in Israel.[42]

Since any of these cases could involve usury, some scholars suggest that Amos is relying in this accusation upon the prohibition of usury in Exod 22:24. The situation depicted in v 11a would be another specific instance of the type of indebtedness described more fully in Amos 2:6b-8.

The Akkadian parallels suggest a different situation than simply (only?) a private debt. During the Neo-Assyrian rule in Mesopotamia, the verb šabāšu and its cognate accusative šibšu referred to regular taxes of corn and straw collected from villages by a provincial government using appointed, local officials. These taxed provisions supplied the provincial government and its central counterpart with staples. The tax rate was usually a straight percentage figured on an "ideal" homer. Records were kept by the central government but the goods themselves were often sent directly to a designated place for storage or consumption. Apart from the fixed percentage sent to the palace, collection and distribution remained in local or regional hands, a situation fraught with potential for graft and corruption.[43]

A similar situation has been suggested for 5:11a independent of the Neo-Assyrian evidence and cognate parallels. Koch believes the accusation concerns a tax rate collected in kind that is causing the small farmer to enter into debt in ever increasing numbers. Moreover, the link with the gate (vs 10, 12) reveals an institutional setting because it was the place for the "decision of all communal affairs." Taxes in kind and the inevitable disputes concerning them would be collected in the gate and adjudicated there.[44]

---

[42]   So Fendler ("Zur Sozialkritik," 37 and note 13); T. N. D. Mettinger, *Solomonic State Officials. A Study of the Civil Government Officials of the Israelite Monarchy* (CB, OTS 5; Lund: C W K Gleerup, 1971) 87, who cites examples of tenant farming in the ancient Near East but is cautious about its relevance for Amos 5:11.

[43]   For these details, see J. N. Postgate, *Taxation and Conscription in the Assyrian Empire* (Rome: Biblical Institute Press, 1974): on šibšu 174-99, taxes, 206-07, records and services owed, 231-36.

[44]   Koch, "Die Entstehung," 246-47.

Fendler supports this general reconstruction as well.[45] According to her the poor, *dallīm*, are citizens who have property and possessions but cannot meet the demands of taxation (exactions) placed upon them. The reference to the rich habitations and vineyards in v 11b are examples of the rewards that accrue to officials involved in collecting state revenue. While based in Samaria, their regional estates come to them as grants from the king in return for services rendered.[46] The relationship between the "poor" and these well-to-do but exacting landowners was at various times a private and an administrative/official one.

Also the term translated "tribute," *maśa'āh* is best understood as a type of exaction. The general meaning of the word is "gift" (Gen 43:34; 2 Sam 11:8; Est 2:18). In addition, it can signify a tax as in 2 Chron 24:6, 9. This latter meaning has the support of cognate parallels.[47]

The interpretation of v 11a as a reference to various forms of official exactions best fits the evidence of the terminology and provides an important reason among several others which explains why the equilibrium of Israel's society was perceived by Amos as unbalanced. Graft in the administration and collection of taxes, or better forced exactions, was *not* the result of insolvency but a direct contribution to it. One cannot say from the evidence of v 11 that what has been reconstructed as a background was either illegal or due to Canaanite influence. Indeed, taxation was a royal privilege and was presupposed as the prerogative (right) of the king even in the anti-monarchical passage of 1 Sam 8:10-18. Perhaps the statement of 1 Sam 8:15, "he will take a tenth of your grain and your vineyards and give it to his officers," reflects the practice of the monarch in Amos' time.[48]

---

45   Fendler, "Zur Sozialkritik," 37-38.

46   See also Chapter Four. Land grants were a favorite method of reward for royal servants in the Neo-Assyrian Empire; J. N. Postgate, *Neo Assyrian royal grants and decrees* (Rome: Biblical Institute Press, 1969).

47   The word also occurs in a list of offerings required by YHWH in Ezek 20:40. For cognate parallels meaning taxes, payments, see C. F. Jean and J. Hoftizer, *Dictionnaire des inscriptions semitiques de l'ouest* (Leiden: E. J. Brill, 1965) 169.

48   Fendler ("Zur Sozialkritik," 37) thinks v 11a concerned a "Zehntabgabe" but surprisingly did not refer to 1 Sam 8:15. From a later

Furthermore, the close connection between the corruption in the administrative processes in the gate (5:10, 12) and the exaction of these payments suggest an overlap among those responsible for both problems. Amos' blistering attack on those who hate the advocate for right in the gate (v 10) implies that his "opponents" were often successful in using or manipulation the administrative process and that the make-up of the local court was either indifferent or powerless in changing course. Finally, one must see in Amos' accusations a concern for the rights of property owners with respect to the various goods they produce or possess, as opposed to excessive exactions, and the right to have their economic dealings fairly adjudicated.

Amos 7:1b

And behold, it was the growth after the king's mowings.

Amos 7:1 begins a series of vision reports which also contain some other material interspersed between the individual reports. Verse 7:1b itself is most likely an explanatory gloss and part of the editorial process. The gloss may be the work of the "Amos school" and formulated early in the editorial process because it clarifies the original agricultural background common to the vision reports.[49]

The term *lekeš* in v 1b can refer either to an agricultural season or its crops. In the present context it refers to the early growth after the spring rains. The point of v 1 is that the locusts arrive at a crucial time; almost nothing has been harvested for the farmer this early in the season because barley and wheat are not yet ripe, yet what has been harvested has gone to the king. Locusts would be a danger after the spring rains as the green crops matured, and during the harvest time proper the main threat would be a fire in the dry fields (7:2, 4; Joel 1:17-20, 2:5). Even if the agricultural year runs its course and ripe fruit is finally gathered, another vision makes it clear to Amos that this signifies nothing more than the "end" for Israel (8:1-2).

---

period, the king's tax of Neh 5:4 is a cause of debt slavery and ruinous mortgages.

[49]   The existence of an "Amos school" as an early editorial committee has been argued by Wolff (*Amos*, 108-11); but he does not attribute 7:1b to their work.

The message of the vision reports, then, is reflective of the agricultural cycle.[50] It is in this context that mention is made of the king's mowings or cuttings *(gizzê hammelek)*. The term "mowings" can refer to the shearings of sheep or the cutting of verdant growth (Ps 72:6). For chronological and contextual reasons, the latter is meant in v 1b.[51] The agricultural context of the first vision report presupposes a time in early spring. Evidently the king claimed the first harvest or gathering of an agricultural year as a tax, perhaps for the support and administration of the affairs of the state (e.g., 1 Kings 4:8-20; 5:7-8). It is difficult to know what crop is referred to in the verse. Because the reference implies a time early in the harvest season, it would probably be wild grass and herbs along with a semi-cultivated hay used for fodder. An early harvest for these crops just after the spring rains would be possible. 1 Kings 18:5 demonstrates that such materials were sought by the king's servants.[52]

The reference to the king's mowings is not formulated as an accusation. As a gloss or even an incidental comment, it demonstrates the fact of prior claims upon a person's property before he/she could make personal use of it. In this particular case, the produce owed to the king was exacted "up front;" i.e., those who contributed the mowings began an agricultural year with an obligation to be met (because of the monarch's prior right) and only subsequent labor and good fortune could meet the remaining personal needs. There is no indication in the vision report itself that such an obligation was burdensome; however, any required payment at the beginning of a harvest season made the later hazards a farmer could face such as locusts, fire and warfare all the more devastating if and when they came.

Amos' occupation and social class could provide insight into the prophet's accusations but not enough information has been preserved for this to be a deciding factor in interpretation. The opinion of generations of scholars is summed up in the description of Amos as "a

---

[50]   S. Talmon, "The Gezer Calendar and the Seasonal Cycle of Ancient Canaan," *JAOS* 83 (1963) 177-87, esp. 184.

[51]   Rudolph, *Amos*, 230.

[52]   Postgate (*Taxation*, 208-10) describes the diligent efforts to secure fodder for the horses belonging to the Assyrian empire. The Romans had a special tax to gather fodder in Syria; see W. R. Smith, *Lectures on the Religion of the Semites* (Edinburgh: A. & C. Black, 1894) 246, note 1.

crude peasant from the half-desolate hills of Tekoa," and a member of the "oppressed classes."[53] Recent scholars have tended to reject this romantic view of a simple shepherd[54] and have stressed among other things the polished poetry of his prophecy. The designation of Amos in the superscription of the book as a *nōqēd* can be related to the reply of Amos to Amaziah in 7:14b--also a secondary tradition--when both statements are understood as a description of some type of herdsman with the responsibilities of procuring supplies as well.[55]

If Amos did hold such a responsible position as this, it does not preclude his personal involvement with those people whose acts aroused his moral outrage. Property-owning classes were adversely affected too by the social circumstances to which Amos reacted. The prophet, however, does not state that he was an advocate for any one group but that he was sent by YHWH to prophesy to the nation. His polemics presuppose a state and local government that have directly contributed to a perceived social imbalance and a corresponding loss of personal property rights for some citizens, specifically with regard to the appropriation of their property.

Hosea

The great variety in the conceptual world of Hebrew prophecy is illustrated by the differences between Amos and Hosea. There is less in Hosea of a sharp critique of economic conditions even though those conditions in his time were probably very similar to those in the previous period under Amos.

The relevant passages in the book of Hosea (4:2a, 5:10a, 7:1d, 12:8-9a) concern property and occur in contexts of accusation and stated reasons for punishment. All but the last passage involve the violation of recognized standards. The last passage (12:8-9a) is included because it refers to a perceived improper accumulation of wealth through economically oppressive means.

---

[53]   The description is that of W. A. Irwin, "The Thinking of Amos," *AJSL* 49 (1932-3) 110, 113.

[54]   So Wolff, *Amos*, 123-24; Rudolph, *Amos*, 96-7. Both scholars provide surveys of various opinions.

[55]   See T. J. Wright's two articles, "Did Amos inspect livers?" *ABR* 23 (1975) 3-11; and "Amos and the 'Sycamore Fig,'" *VT* 26 (1976) 362-68.

Hosea 4:2a

(There is) deceit and murder and theft and adultery.

The judgment speech in Hos 4:1-3 draws attention to the relationship between the "mourning" of creation and the lack of the ethical practices which Hosea claims make up the "knowledge of God."[56] In fact, v 2 lists the negative counterparts of this knowledge. Whether Hosea draws on the decalogue or not in this passage is disputed,[57] even though certain of the negative practices cited are also cited in the decalogue,[58] and in both passages (Hos 4:1; Exod 20:1) the introduction refers to the word(s) of YHWH. Theft and adultery are crimes against a man's possessions--his property and wife--as can be deceit *(kahēš)* and even murder. Deceit means not just lying but also defrauding someone.[59] There is no clue in the passage to a social setting for these crimes.

Hosea 5:10a

The Judaean officials are like those who remove a boundary marker.

Removal of a boundary marker is prohibited in the legal and wisdom traditions (Deut 19:14; 27:17; Job 24:2; Prov 22:28, 23:10). Both of these traditions recognize that such markers were used to preserve family property inherited from ancestors.[60]

---

56   H. W. Wolff, "'Wissen um Gott' bei Hosea als Urform der Theologie," *EvT* 12 (1952/3) 533-54; M. J. Buss, *The Prophetic Word of Hosea: A Morphological Study* (BZAW 111; Berlin: A Topelmann, 1969) 106.

57   A negative conclusion is reached by D. W. Nowack, *Die Kleinen Propheten* (HAT; Göttingen: Vandenhoeck & Ruprecht, 1897) 30. A positive conclusion is reached by W. Rudolph, *Hosea* (KAT 13/1; Gütersloh: Gerd Mohn, 1966) 100-101, 162.

58   *rṣḥ*= Exod 20:13; *gnb* = 20:15; *n'p*= 20:14.

59   Wolff, *Hosea* (Hermeneia; Philadelphia: Fortress Press, 1974) 67-8; and Hos 7:3, 10:13; Lev 5:21f. See also B. S. Jackson, *Theft in Early Jewish Law* (Oxford: Clarendon Press, 1972) 55.

60   Deut. 19:14; Prov 22:28.

Hosea employs a simile in accusing Judaean officials of committing acts "like" (k) those who remove a marker. The references to the preservation of family property with a marker[61] is used for comparison in accord with the intention of a simile. Probably the real issue involved territory occupied by Judaean troops led by certain "officials," *šārīm*, during border warfare.

Hosea 7:1d

The thief enters (in), the robber-band raids without.

The thief and the robber-band (*gedûd*) illustrate two types of misappropriation often distinguished in ancient societies.[62] The distinction is between the thief who was usually a member of the community and the robber or brigand who was frequently an outsider. In the context of v 1, these examples are cited as evidence of Ephraim/Samaria's falsehood. The mention of a "robber-band" is possibly a reference to one of several groups vying for power in the last years of the northern kingdom or to a band of brigands during this same period. On the other hand, the charge of misappropriation is lodged against Ephraim/Samaria and the following three verses of chapter 7 concern evil deeds[63] that please the royal house. Perhaps the charge of robber-band is lodged against the royal house and its associates for what is perceived as brigandage.

Hosea 12:8-9a

Canaan, (in) his hand are false scales, He loves to oppress.
Ephraim said, 'How I am rich, I have gained wealth.'

---

61   F. C. Fensham, "Common Trends in Curses of the Near Eastern Treaties and KUDURRU-Inscriptions Compared with Maledictions of Amos and Isaiah," *ZAW* 75 (1963) 155-75. For some other ancient Near Eastern parellels see, "The Teaching of Amenemope," *ANET* 421, and the adjurations of a "Shurpu" text in W. Beyerlin (ed.), *Near Eastern Religious Texts Relating to the Old Testament* (Philadelphia: Westminster Press, 1978) 132.

62   Jackson, *Theft*, 9-11.

63   The method of composition and the relationship of the individual units in 7:1-7 are obscure; see Wolff, *Hosea*, 108-10.

Verse 9a provides the clue that Ephraim is addressed as Canaan in v 8. The appellative Canaan(ite) is used in this passage as a synonym for trader or merchant,[64] and is designed to evoke unflattering images of the merchant. Thus the term is *not* evidence for the corrupt economic influence of any ethnic or religious group. No details are given about commercial conditions except a charge of fraud by using false scales, evidently a common accusation during this time period (Amos 8:5; Mic 6:11). Both legal and wisdom traditions were concerned over the employment of false weights and scales to defraud a person involved in trade.[65]

Hosea is not addressing merchants but Ephraim who is made to boast that he has gained riches. The accusation of fraud against Ephraim, as in a similar charge in 7:1, suggests that perhaps certain types of fiscal or commercial policies are perceived by the prophet as economic oppression (*ʿāšaq*).[66] In this respect the prophet's accusation is similar to that of Amos in 3:9-10. Unfortunately, nothing more specific can be determined from the context.

Isaiah

The following passages in the book of Isaiah are relevant to the present discussion: 3:12-15b, 5:8, 10:1-2. Each passage is concerned with the acquisition of property and occurs in the context of accusations about the ethical nature of such appropriation. The acquisitions op property, whether the latter is movable (3:14) or immovable (5:8), are actually perceived as misappropriation and violations of the owner's rights.

Isaiah 3:12, 13-15b

My people's taskmasters deal cruelly *(meʿôlēl)*, And userers *(nōšîm)* rule them.

---

64   Job 40:30; Prov 31:24; Isa 23:8; Zech 11:7, 11; Ezek 16:29.

65   Deut 25:13-15; Lev 19:35-36; Prov 11:1, 20:23; Ezek 45:10. See also the "Teaching of Amenemope," *ANET*, 388; and the "Negative Confession of Sin." in Beyerlin, *Religious Texts*, 66.

66   See Mic 6:16a, which is more explicit in its condemnation of state fiscal and economic policies.

'My people, your leaders take you astray, and confuse the way
of your paths.'
YHWH has taken his place to contend,
He stands to judge (the) peoples.
YHWH comes for judgment with the elders and officials of his
people;
'You have depastured the vineyard, spoil from the poor is in your
houses.
What do you mean by crushing my people, And grinding the face
of the poor?

Isaiah 3 contains various units of prophetic speech which have
been arranged to illustrate the dissolution of Judaean society. Verse 12
precedes a prophetic speech reflective of legal procedure.[67] These two
units (12, 13-15) are joined because of their common theme of
economic oppression.

Not only is it probable that v 12 was originally independent from
vs 13-15, but it is possible that the verse is composite. The use of
suffixes is not consistent, yet the alternation between the third and
second person usage is intelligible in context. Textual problems have
produced two main interpretations of the verse with varying
translations. (1) The first interpretation finds in *meʿôlēl* and *nāšīm*
references to child(ren) and women respectively, so that v 12a becomes
a sarcastic comment about national leadership,[68] as in a similar
statement in Isa 3:4. (2) A second interpretation follows the LXX,[69]

---

[67]   H. J. Boecker, *Redeformen des Rechtsleben im Alten Testament*
(WMANT 14; Neukirchen-Vluyn: Neukirchener Verlag, 1964) 84.

[68]   Some scholars read the singular *meʿôlēl* as a possible reference
to the king, deriving the word from *ʿll* "to be or act like a child;" so B.
Duhm, *Jesaia* (HAT; Göttingen: Vandenhoeck & Ruprecht, 1902) 24-25.

[69]   *laós mou, oi praktores umōn kalamōntai umas, kai oi
apaitountes kurieousin umōn.* The *praktores* was an official concerned
with taxes and the collection of debts. The Greek word translates the
Hebrew *ngśym*, itself a derogatory term for leadership. The Hebrew can
mean taskmaster (Exod 3:7, 5:6, 10, 13), or an exactor of taxes (2 Kings
23:35), or one who demands payment of a debt (Deut 15:2-3). The verb
apaiteo, "to demand," apparently renders the Hebrew *nśym* as a participle
from *nśh* a verb used several times for creditor and usury in the Hebrew

either completely or in part, and finds in v 12ab a charge of usury against leaders, probably a complaint about financial misappropriation and taxes. The second interpretation makes more sense in the present context.[70] The difference between the two interpretations is based essentially on the vowel points of *nšym*, whereby the second interpretation follows the Greek text which seems to presuppose *nōšīm* (userers).

The placing of v 12 as a preface to the trial-speech of vs 13-15 supports the second interpretation, because the common denominator is economic oppression by the nation's leaders. The accusations in v 12 give no specifics for the charge of cruelty and usury, but the context of official oppression implies a broader understanding for the charge of usury[71] (and mistreatment) than the simple taking of interest on a loan. Perhaps various state and local exactions are in the prophet's mind. Describing one's leaders as taskmasters lends support to this suggestion. Furthermore, the charge of goods accumulation against the elders and officials in v 14 may be intended as an illustration of cruelty and usury.

The elders and officials of YHWH's people are accused of "depasturing" (*bʿr*)[72] the vineyard. The same verb is used in Exod 22:4 to describe the action of an animal that has broken into a cultivated field and eaten the crop belonging to another person. This is the sense of the verb in v 14ba (cf. Isa 5:5). The corresponding phrase of v 14bb implies that the vineyard be thought of in terms of its produce and the right of its owner(s) to possession of its produce as well as in terms of

---

Bible. See Exod 22:24; Deut 15:2, 24:11; 2 Kings 4:1; Jer 15:10; Neh 5:10-11.

[70]   In agreement with G. B. Gray, *Isaiah 1-27* (ICC; New York: Charles Scribner's Sons, 1912) 67-68; O. Kaiser, *Isaiah 1-12* (OTL; Philadelphia: Westminster Press, 1972) 43-44; and H. Wildberger, *Jesaja* (BKAT 10; Neukirchen-Vluyn: Neukirchener Verlag, 1972) 129. Both Kaiser and Wildberger follow the interpretation of the LXX and derive *meʿôlēl* from ʿll, "to glean or mistreat."

[71]   For studies of usury in the Hebrew Bible, see E. Neufeld, "The Prohibition Against Loans at Interest in Ancient Hebrew Laws,"*HUCA* 26 (1955) 355-412; H. Gamoran, "The Biblical Law Against Loans on Interest," *JNES* 30 (1971) 127-34; R. P. Maloney, "Usury and Restrictions on Interest-Taking in the Ancient Near East," *CBQ* 36 (1974) 1-20.

[72]   The translation "depasture" is taken from Gray (*Isaiah*, 68-9).

a metaphor for YHWH's people. The verb *gzl* means to "rob" and the cognate noun found in v 14b is used in a corresponding sense.[73] Elders and officials,[74] i.e., those responsible for the maintenance of order, have in their houses the possessions of the poor. The whole tenor of vs 12-15, especially with 'their' emphasis on the leaders of society, suggests it is precisely the official status of their position which has resulted in the perceived (mis)appropriation of property. It is difficult to determine whether this is only the result of "official" pressure and exactions or if certain private transactions are included as well.[75]

The collection of produce from the poor and its storage in the houses of others has parallels in Amos 3:9-11, Mic 6:10 and Jer 5:26-28. In the Jeremiah passage, not only are the houses of the oppressors full of treachery *(mirmāh)* but men are caught like birds in a trap, so that probably acts of foreclosure and certainly debt slavery are in the prophet's mind.

Isaiah 5:8

Woe to those who join house to house, who add field to field;
Until there is no further place,
And you dwell alone in the midst of the land.

This is the first accusation in a series of "woe" speeches.[76] The first speech (5:8-10) is structured like a prophetic judgment speech and concludes with YHWH's announcement about the future. The impersonal participial form in the accusation is not a "general and

---

[73]   According to B. Jackson (*Theft*, 4-5, 109), the prophets use *gzl* in the more restricted sense of "economic exploitation." See further Isa 10:2; Mic 2:2, 3:2; Ezek 18:7.

[74]   Bibliography and a discussion of these two groups can be found in F. Frick, *The City in Ancient Israel* (SBLDS 36; Missoula, Scholars Press, 1977) 116-24. It is their function as national leaders that is in question in this passage. In Isa 1:23 the *śārīm*(officials) are called "companions of thieves" and accused of perverting justice.

[75]   Probably both are involved. See the comments on Amos 5:11, *supra.*

[76]   On woe speeches, see W. Janzen,*Mourning Cry and Woe Oracle* (BZAW 125; Berlin: Walter de Gruyter, 1972); C. Hardmeier, *Texttheorie und biblische Exegese: Zur rhetorischen Funktion der Trauermetaphorik in der Prophetie* (BET 79; Münich: Chr. Kaiser, 1978).

timeless indictment" because the relationship between the "indictment" and the coming judgment is too specific.[77]

Latifundia, or large estates, could become regional monopolies in a rural setting. No injunction against such a venture is quoted in this passage although other biblical traditions exist which speak to the issue. For instance, the Deuteronomistic presentation of the conquest highlights the giving of the land to Israel and its apportionment to the people as YHWH's gracious act. There are antecedents to this thought which are at least as old as Isaiah and almost certainly older (Deut 32:8-9; Ps 68:10-11; Hos 8:1), which would impede the process of land monopoly. Concern for boundary markers and one's inheritance *(nahalāh)* also protected the equilibrium and economic viability of agricultural communities.[78]

It is generally true to say that land was the capital of antiquity.[79] Sale contracts from various civilizations in the ancient Near East make it abundantly clear that the sale of immovable property was closely witnessed. Some scholars have suggested that a development in the use of "liquid" capital (silver, gold) by the eighth century in Judah made the purchase of immovable property easier for an entrepreneur.[80] While a new "money economy" *may* have made the growth of landed estates more frequent, the poor harvest announced in the name of YHWH (v 10) implies that the wealth sought by the estate owners was produce (on the assumption that the punishment announced fits the crime!). Moreover, the "sale" of property often presupposed by scholars from v 8 would probably not have been the result of an attractive financial offer but a sale made out of necessity. Indeed, the emphasis of the "woe" is on the acquisition of property, its actual sale is nowhere mentioned.

More was at stake than simple ownership of house and property. Participation in the cultic life of Judah required the presentation of tithes and offerings so that the loss of house and field would be

---

[77]   Against E. Gerstenberger, "The Woe Oracles of the Prophets," *JBL* 81 (1962) 252. Note the change in the passage from third person to second person (direct address).

[78]   See Chapter Two.

[79]   Carney, *The Economics of Antiquity*, 20.

[80]   Kaiser, *Isaiah*, 65; H. Bardtke, "Die Latifundien in Juda während der zweite Hälfte des achten Jahrhunderts v. Chr. (zum Verständnis von Jes 5, 8-10)," *Hommages a Andre Dupont-Sommer* (ed. A. Caquot et al.; Paris: Adrien Maisonneuve, 1971) 239.

humiliating to a former owner who could no longer meet his previous sacral obligations.[81] The sale of a home and fields would mean loss of civil privileges (rights) as well. The property owner was the full citizen entitled to what Köhler summarized as the four great rights: marriage, cult, war and the administration of justice.[82] The loss of citizenship is envisaged in 8b where a shift is made to the second person and direct address. Wildberger brings this out in his translation, "yet you alone live as citizens*(Vollbürger)* in the midst of the land."[83] The loss of the rights of a property owner meant a probable further imbalance in communal affairs and in the economic structure of the community. There is no indication (v 8) of the culprits' identity, yet it is difficult to view these circumstances as only a local imbalance. This woe speech has certain similarities with the preaching of Amos where corruption had a central and urban base.[84] The *latifundia*-lords easily fit the description of the exacting taskmasters (3:12) or corrupt officials (1:23, 3:14, 10:1-2), so that a search for culprits should start with

---

[81]   Duhm (*Jesaia*, 34) points out this close connection between the ownership of property and the religious/cultic life of a family.

[82]   This is the formulation of L. Köhler, "Justice in the Gate," *Hebrew Man* (Nashville: Abingdon Press, 1956) 130. It has been suggested that the tenth commandment of the decalogue was designed to protect the citizenship rights of the property owner; so A Phillips, *Ancient Israel's Criminal Law* (Oxford: Basil Blackwell, 1970) 149-52. It is difficult, however, to agree with his contention that the decalogue was Israel's pre-exilic criminal code regardless of the merits of this particular suggestion.

[83]   Wildberger, *Jesaja*, 175. He finds in the hophal of *yšb* the meaning "mit allen öffentlichen Rechten und Pflichten ausgestattet im Lande ansässig sein (183)." Building on earlier studies, N. Gottwald has cited repeated instances where this verb and its cognate noun means to rule or have authority; see his *Tribes of Yahweh*, 512-20.

[84]   R. Fey, *Amos und Jesaja. Abhangigkeit und Eigenstandigkeit des Jesaja* (WMANT 12; Neukirchen-Vluyn: Neukirchener Verlag, 1963) 60-61. He argues that Isa 5:8-10 is dependent on Amos 5:11-12a, 3:15b, 6:11. Similarity of circumstances with similar reactions are more probable.

them.[85] As will be demonstrated in Chapter Four these officials had certain property rights which would have given them an advantage in acquiring new land.

Isaiah 10:1-2

Woe to those who make evil statutes,
And the writers who write suffering;
To turn aside the poor from justice,
And to rob the poor of my people of their right;
To make widows their spoil, and the fatherless their plunder.

One way that houses and fields were acquired is illustrated by this passage. The word pair *ḥqq-ktb* is employed in Job 19:23 and Isa 30:8, both times in the context of recording a message for others to read. The MT should be retained over any emendations.[86]

A more difficult question concerns the audience of the woe speech; was it the northern kingdom, as the connection with 9:7-20 suggests, or has editorial work separated it from another series of woe speeches in Chapter 5? The reference to "my people" in v 2a implies Judah.[87]

The traditional accusations in v 2 have parallels in other passages. The verb *nṭh* in the legal metaphor of "turning aside the poor" *(lehaṭṭôt dallīm)* also occurs in the similar contexts of Amos 2:7 and Isa 29:21, as does the use of the verb "rob"*(gzl)* in a cognate form in Isa 3:14 and Mic 2:2. Protection of the widow and orphan was a universal concern in the ancient Near East.[88] The prophet elsewhere (1:23) refers to widows and orphans as victims of officials *(śārīm)* who pervert justice

---

85   Against Bardtke ("Die Latifundien," 244-50), who argues that the dissolution and fall of the northern kingdom drove military personnel, rich refugees and traders into Judah under Hezekiah's reign, and that the capital brought with them upset the economy. Isa 2:6b-7 is his textual evidence and the passage will hardly bear the weight he assigns to it.

86   Schwantes *(Das Recht,* 102-03) provides a thorough analysis of the variant readings and opts for the MT.

87   So Wildberger, *Jesaja,* 180-83.

88   F. C. Fensham, "Widow, Orphan and the Poor in Ancient Near Eastern Legal and Wisdom Literature," *JNES* 21 (1962) 129-30.

due these weaker members of society for economic gain. A similar situation is obviously pictured in the woe speech of 10:1-2.

The making/writing of statutes probably does not refer to the making of laws in the modern sense but to the recording of decisions and rulings brought for arbitration to judges, or as a reference to those persons who administrate "statutes" *(ḥōq)* concerning the will of the crown (Gen 47:26; Num 27:11; 1 Sam 30:25). It has been argued that an office is disparagingly referred to in v 1, which is an adaptation of a premonarchic office connected with tribal warfare, the levy, and the apportionment of land.[89] The early poetry of Israel contains references to this office(r) entitled *meḥōqēq* (Judg 5:9, 14; Deut 33:21; Num 21:18; cf. Ps 60:8-11). Under the monarchies, various officials with this title and perhaps others as well probably functioned in these same capacities. They were also concerned with the administration of justice (Prov 8:15-16, 31:4-5) and, as Isa 10:1-2 demonstrates, the proper administration of property rights. While Isa 10:1-2 may presuppose an office similar to that reconstructed by Hentschke, it seems less than certain that this is the case. It does seem correct, however, to agree with him and others that some form of administrative and official compliance would be necessary for these "evil statutes" to be enacted.[90]

Similar terminology to that of v 1-2 is also found in the account of Jeremiah's purchase of his cousin's field. In the sealed deed of purchase are contained "terms and conditions" previously agreed to (Jer 32:11). The conditions *(ḥûqqīm)* are also obligations as well. In the Isaianic woe, the conditions are perceived as suffering and robbery, not judicious and fair.

This woe speech is an important passage because it shows the close relationship between the legal/administrative process and the loss of property rights. Statutes that would only be agreed to under duress were forced upon the poor. It should be noted that in this passage, as in the book of Amos, the poor are not propertyless but victims of a system that could appropriate their possessions through the statutory process and the use of contract/deed documents. The prophet's bitter description of the "conditions" suggests the "rights" of the appropriator or purchaser received more consideration than those of the seller. Administrators involved in such a system almost certainly benefited

---

89   R. Hentschke, *Satzung und Setzender* (BWANT 3; Stuttgart: W. Kolhammer, 1963) 11-20.
90   Wildberger, *Jesaja*, 198.

materially (either directly or indirectly) from the imposition of these regulations.[91]   Also, the statutes themselves almost certainly dealt with such things as the sale and transfer of property, foreclosure and confiscation of collateral, and conditions for servitude/debt slavery.[92]

The legality of these statutes is seemingly not in question, nor is there any question of a Canaanite influence on the making of these conditions as suggested by Fey.[93]   The statutes are assumed by the prophet to be legal and Judaean. It is their effect that evokes the cry of woe and the expectation of future punishment (10:3-4). In fact, what is now called "casuistic law" in the legal corpora of the Pentateuch most likely derived some of its material from similar *Sitze im Leben* where a ruling or custom became codified. Only a fraction of case decisions and possible precedents have been preserved in the Hebrew Bible, especially with regard to commercial practices and their corresponding statutes or even ideal cases used for examples.[94]   Obviously the prophet perceived a great difference between the traditional claim that the poor should be protected by the community and the commercial practices of his own community which resulted in the robbery of their "rights."   If the perception were accurate, the basic social institutions of Judaean society no longer mediated YHWH's will and the prophet proclaimed that they must suffer the consequences.

The violators of citizens' property rights are named by title or specifically alluded to in 3:12, 14 and 10:1. In each instance the culprits appear to have used official positions of influence for the acquisition of property (cf. Isa 1:23 as well). The prophet opposes their exacting and acquiring measures as infringement and cruelty without stating any reason for opposition except that of YHWH's displeasure.

---

91   "Can a throne of destruction be allied with you (*i.e.*, YHWH), that devises misfortune by statute*(ḥōq)?"* (Ps 94: 20).

92   On statutes, see further discussion under Mic 6:16a; *infra*.

93   Fey (*Amos und Jesaja*, 62-63, note 4) thinks the prophet is inspired by Amos 2:6-8 and is also opposing casuistic law (of Canaanite origin and profane). It is not casuistic law as such that is opposed but the effects of individual cases and rulings. See the comments on Amos 2:6b-8, *supra*.

94   M. J. Buss, "The Distinction Between Civil and Criminal Law in Ancient Israel," *Proceedings of the Sixth World Congress of Jewish Studies* (Jerusalem: Academic Press, 1977) 1. 55.

Micah

Isaiah's younger contemporary, Micah,[95] lived in rural Judah where his sharp criticism of society led Cornill to write, "in him Amos lives again."[96] His descriptions of Judaean society as a whole are indeed similar to those concerning Israel in the book of Amos. An obvious reason for this is that the two states had much in common.

The following verses in the book of Micah are relevant to this study and singled out for analysis: 2:1-2, 2:8b-9, and 6:16a. Each of these texts are accusations and/or stated reasons for displeasure with regard to the misuse of property. There are additional allusions and terminology in the book which provide aid in interpreting these texts and references to them appear at appropriate points.

Micah 2:1-2

Woe to those who plot iniquity, and work evil on their beds.
In the light of morning they do it,
Because it is within their power to do so.
They desire fields so they rob them, and houses so they take them away;
They oppress a man and his house, Even a man and his inheritance.

The woe speech of Mic 2:1-5 has the two-part structure of a judgment speech with the reasons for woe (vs 1-2) followed by an announcement of future judgment (vs 3-5). The culprits are described in impersonal style rather than named by title or position as in 3:1; yet there is undoubtedly much overlap between the two groups.

The reference in v 1ba to dawn is not incidental. As Köhler pointed out, local assemblies probably met in the gate at this time to

---

[95]   Recent scholarship with older bibliography includes H. W. Wolff, "Micah the Moreshite-The Prophet and His Background," *Israelite Wisdom: Theological and Literary Essays in Honor of Samuel Terrien* (ed. J. G. Gammie, *et al*; New York: Union Theological Seminary, 1978) 78-84; and K. Jeppesen, "New Aspects of Micah Research," *JSOT* 8 (1978) 3-32.

[96]   C. H. Cornill, *The Prophets of Israel* (Chicago: Open Court, 1913) 69.

conduct the affairs of the community.[97] Dawn was a time when those
going out to the fields could assemble before leaving the village. The
idiom of v 1bb, literally, "because god/power is in their hand," seems
to have a legal connotation implying a right or prerogative (cf. Gen
31:29)[98] and thus is compatible with a social setting of legal procedure
in the gate of a village. Those who plot iniquity bring their plans to
completion through the administrative process because they have some
claim of legal precedent or justification for what they do, probably
referring to foreclosure proceedings and evictions (2:2, 9). If the
culprits are also those responsible for the oversight of communal affairs
and who draw their legal prerogative partly from their office--like the
heads and rulers of 3:1, 9-- then property appropriation in this reference
had an official character and backing, possibly with royally designated
authority.

These acts of appropriation are described by the prophets as robbery
and oppression using terminology associated with theft of property.[99]
Such acts or even the desire to commit them break the ethical norms of
Israel's legal traditions (Exod 20:17; Deut 5:18).[100] The expansion of
the tenth commandment in Exod 20:17 is evidence that a "house"

---

[97]   Köhler ("Justice in the Gate," 130-31) using Zeph 3:5 as a
textual reference. We should add that early morning appears to be the
time of assembly described in Ruth 3:13-14, 4:1f. See also Jer 21:12a
where the house of David is commanded to "do justice in the morning,
deliver the person robbed (*gazûl*) from the hand of the oppressor (*'ôšāq*)."

[98]   As *paterfamilias*, Laban claims to Jacob in Gen 31:29a that he
has, so to speak, "the right to do him evil" because of the latter's theft.
Boecker (*Redeformen*, 41-45) has shown in some detail that the whole
passage (Gen 31:25-42) gives examples of customary legal procedures
and speech in a dispute. Laban's claim to have *'ēl* in the hand is the
claim of customary or legal right to do Jacob harm (*rā'*), exactly the term
used in Mic 2:1a to describe those who do "evil." Apparently, the idiom
of Mic 2:1b and Gen 31:29a had a legal *Sitz im Leben* as an expression
of a person's power or prerogative according to legal standards and
practice.

[99]   *Supra*, Amos, note 34; Isaiah, note 73.

[100]   The verb *ḥmd* in Exod 20:17 is thought to have the significance
of acquisition as well as desire. For a defense of the view that Exod
20:17 refers to "coveting" see B. Jackson, "Liability for Intention in
Early Jewish Law," in his *Essays in Jewish and Comparative Legal
History* (SJLA 10; Leiden: E. J. Brill, 1975) 202-34.

included possessions, and perhaps reflects the fact that without them one loses the privileges of citizenship as well. While such ethical norms may have provided a source of accusation for the prophet, the second chapter contains other references to land ownership and property rights which may have influenced Micah as well.

The phrase in 2:2b, "a man and his house, a man and his inheritance," is one references that has been described by Alt as early Israel's social ideal[101] and a basis for Micah's critique. He understands the term *naḥalāh* to refer to an earlier Israelite concept of inalienable family property (1 Kings 21:3; Prov 19:4; cf. Lev 25:23). Moreover, he related the ideal to the order of free Israelite peasant-farmers who, for religious and cultic reasons, kept the sabbath year agricultural laws in the transition from seminomadism to an agrarian economy and who also redivided tribal property by lot periodically.[102] According to Alt, Mic 2:1-5 is a witness to the temporary overthrow of this sacral order by the *latifundia*-lords in the capital city of Jerusalem. After YHWH's judgment on Jerusalem--which is actually a separate city-state--Judah will be reconstituted and the land again redistributed according to ancient customs. Beyerlin's monograph on Micah[103] is in substantial agreement with Alt' proposals but supplements his views by proposing that Micah's ethical basis was founded on the older amphictyonic laws which were proclaimed at an annual ceremony of covenant renewal to celebrate the maintenance of this sacral order.

Several aspects of this influential reconstruction deserve assessment. The high value that an agrarian community would place on a citizen and his/her inheritance of immovable property is almost self-evident, for some such value would provide protection and stability for family production. That this evaluation of property rights for a family was buttressed by theological tenets in Israel, such as the insistence that it was founded on YHWH's will and protection, is clearly seen in the protests of the eighth-century prophets. With this much Alt and Beyerlin would agree. On the other hand, there is insufficient evidence for a periodic, communal redistribution of land in

---

101   *Supra.*, Introduction, and Chapter Two.
102   Alt, "Der Anteil," 369-70; *ibid.*, "Micha 2, 1-5. "*G e s Anadasmos* in Juda," *Kl Schr* III, 373-81.
103   Beyerlin, *Die Kulttradition Israels*, 57-9.

the Hebrew Bible, Mic 2:5 and Ps 16:6 notwithstanding.[104] The evidence, as Mic 2:2b seems to presuppose, is that of familial control of agriculturally productive plots with corresponding obligations toward the village/clan.[105] Finally, there is little reason to agree with Alt (and others) that Micah opposed Jerusalem as a city-state separate from his beloved Judah. As the capital of Judah, the city's influence was extensive in the Shephelah, but Micah's critique extended to the nation and not just the city's officials or the separate entity of Judah.[106] Alt's theory reflects his view of a cultural dualism in Judah where the city-state of Jerusalem was not only the private property of the Davidic dynasty but also dominated by Canaanite social practices abhorrent to the more conservative Judaean citizenry. There is nothing in Micah's, or in Isaiah's prophecy,[107] that points to Canaanite responsibility for the acts of Judaean officials (Mic 3:1, 9). There is no evidence either for a thoroughgoing dualism between Jerusalem and Judah in the book of Micah.

Micah 2:8b, 9

From off the clothing they strip the cloak...
The women of my people you drive from their beloved homes,
From their children you take my glory forever.

---

[104]   The date, background and significance of Mic 2:5 is disputed. We agree with the interpretation of W. Rudolph, *Micha-Nahum, Habakuk-Zephanje*(KAT 13/3; Gütersloh: Gerd Mohn, 1975) 55 and note 13. Verse 5 refers to a one-time redistribution of the land that is expected in the future and is perhaps modelled on the traditions about the first distribution of the land under Joshua. It has been argued that much of Mic 2:3-5 was expanded during the exile; see J. Jeremias, "Die Deutung der Gerichtsworte Michas in der Exilzeit," *ZAW* 83 (1971) 333-35.

[105]   For details, see Chapter Two.

[106]   G. Buccellati, *Cities and Nations of Ancient Syria* (Studi Semitici; Rome: University of Rome, 1967) 170-81, has also criticized Alt on this point. Elsewhere (pp. 195-238), Buccellati has a penetrating critique of Alt's theories of dualism in both Israel and Judah.

[107]   The reference to a righteous Jerusalem as at the beginning in Isa 1:26 may, in fact, even refer to the Canaanite past of the city!

Micah 2:3-11 has so many textual problems that any reconstruction is uncertain at points.[108] Verse 6 presents Micah in conflict with certain people who oppose his message and at the same time provides a context with which to understand the verses that immediately follow.[109]

Micah 2:8b is a difficult text where seemingly the loss of a cloak is described as having been stripped away from the person wearing it. According to Exod 22:8, a dispute over clothing can become a criminal matter. Also, in Exod 22:26-27 it is forbidden to take a garment overnight in pledge. This latter reference may provide the rationale for the crime described in 2:8b; it is an attempt to force compliance over some contractual agreement by the seizure of a garment. The verb *pšṭ* ("strip") in v 8b is the same term twice used by the prophet in 3:2b-4 to make the charge of cannibalism. Evidently the garment--whether it was a pledge for collateral or not--was violently seized and provided the prophet with a graphic illustration.

The process of property appropriation is described further by v 9. The mention of women and children but not men as the objects of eviction (*grš*, cf. Ezek 45:9) suggests the reference is to widows and orphans.[110] Such people may not have had a steady source of income but still possessed the family property or what is described as their "beloved" houses. They would also lack adequate representation in the gate assemblies for communal affairs,[111] making them particularly vulnerable to creditors and oppression. Thus they are driven out of their homes and the children lose their glory forever.[112] The clash over the property rights of the evictors and the children is evident from the

---

[108]   The translation of 2:8b, 9 follows the MT except for reading plural suffixes in v 9.

[109]   A. van der Woude, "Micah in Dispute with the Pseudo-Prophets," *VT* 19 (1969) 246-48. Micah's opponents are not just prophets but, where specifically alluded to (2:1-2, 3:1, 9), are citizens with a great deal of economic power as well.

[110]   *Supra.*, note 88

[111]   It is stated in Exod 22:24 that YHWH protects such people as widows and orphans. This statement probably reflects the fact that men and property owners alone comprised the local administrative assemblies.

[112]   Is this emphasis on forever (*leʿōlam*) a bitter acknowledgment that sabbatical year measures or other ameliorating practices (*gōʾēl*) will be ignored with regard to debts; or perhaps that they do not exist?

terminology. What seems to involve a simple case of eviction concerns the loss of glor *(hādār)* as well. According to Ezek 16:6-14, the concluding act of establishment in the land is described as the people's "glory" and as YHWH's gift.[113] In Mic 2:9, the loss of property for the children becomes a loss of what YHWH had granted to "my people." This reference is another instance (cf. comments on 2:1-2) where the prophet's conception of landed property is revealed. In this particular case, land is described as glory because it is viewed as part of YHWH's gift to his people

The verdict of Mic 2:10 is that the evictors acquired no place of "rest" *(menûḥāh).* This word is also used for the heritage of the land in Deut 12:9 and Ps 95:11. It is hard to miss the irony in this verse; the prophet employs the work "rest" as a *double entendre* saying that another person's property is no resting place for the greedy whose actions lead, as the verse concludes, to destruction.[114] The use of *menûḥāh* for the property is additional evidence for the prophet's understanding of the land in terms of YHWH's gift.

The judgment speech against the heads and rulers[115] of the nation (3:1-4, 9-12) contains two accusations, both of which relate directly to the understanding of 2:1-2, 8b, 9. (1) They do not know (practice) justice and (2) they are cannibals. The first charge relates to their responsibilities to administer communal affairs and more specifically

---

113   See also Ezek 20:6; Jer 3:19; 2 Sam 14:16.

114   L. Allen, *Joel, Obadiah, Jonah and Micah* (NICOT; Grand Rapids: Eerdmans, 1976) 298. The root word for destruction *(ḥbl)* in v 10 has a homonym meaning "pledge," leading Mays *(Micah,* 72) to conclude that the original text was an accusation against the creditors, "you pledge with a ruinous pledge." It is a plausible reconstruction in the context of Mic 2:8-10, but his overall understanding of this verse requires additional emendations that make his view improbable. The MT of v 10b is perhaps evidence of paronomasia as is the reference to *menûḥāh* in 10a.

115   The word pair *rōʾš* and *qāṣîn* occurs in Judg 11:11 and is used in describing Jephtah's position as the military leader of Gilead. The functions of the *rōʾšîm* in Israel were military and judicial; so J. Bartlett, "The use of the word *rʾš* a title in the Old Testament," *VT* 19 (1969) 2-4. E. Hammershaimb, "Some Leading Ideas in the Book of Micah," *Some Aspects of Old Testament Prophecy from Isaiah to Malachi* (Copenhagen: Rosenkilde og Bagger, 1966) 31-32, thinks these titles must refer to royal administrative appointees.

the court system. The second is a metaphor. The terminology employed in the description of dismemberment and robbery clearly implies that economic oppression and the loss of possessions are the real charge.[116]

Micah 6:16a

Omri's statutes are kept,
All the deeds of Ahab's house you follow.

This accusation concludes a passage comprised of utterances assigned differing dates and authorship (6:9-16).[117] The familiar charge of commercial thievery in vs 10-12 is followed by an extended announcement of judgment. The subject matter of the passage is socio-economic in nature so that the specific reference to statutes in v 16 must concern such matters as well. Elsewhere, kings and officials did uphold statutes in this realm of affairs (1 Sam 30:25; Isa 10:1-2; Ps 94:20).[118]

Economic expansion in Israel reached its peak under the Omride dynasty as a result of lucrative trading and commercial alliances.[119] The accusation of v 16a probably reflects awareness of changes in domestic economic policies effected by the dynasty in conjunction with its larger commercial relationships of international trade. Royal greed in the acquisition of Naboth's vineyard was attributed to the Omride Ahab (1 Kings 21:1-16) and may even be alluded to in the reference to the works of his house. The Judaean royal house and/or its

---

[116]   Wolff ("Micah," 79) thinks instead that the mistreatment of conscripted workers is in the prophet's mind as in 3:10.

[117]   Wolff ("Micah," 77) is probably correct that the passage comes from Micah with the possible exception of v 9b. The accusations of vs 10-12 are common in the eighth century and v 16a presupposses political autonomy.

[118]   Hentschke (*Satzung*, 89-90) attributes the verse to deuteronomistic circles. The DtrH, however, castigates the Omrides primarily in terms of religious apostasy (1 Kings 16:25-26). This passage (Mic 6:9-16) concerns socio-economic crimes.

[119]   J. M. Miller, "The Elisha Cycle and the Accounts of the Omride Wars," *JBL* 85 (1966) 441-54, esp. 443; and B. Peckham, "Israel and Phoenicia," *Magnalia Dei* (ed. F. M. Cross et al.; Garden City: Doubleday & Co., 1976) 236-37.

representatives are accused of following the example of Israel's economic policies through the enforcement of certain statutes *(ḥuqqôt)*. The accusation does not support the view of massive Canaanite influence in Judah, as several recent scholars have opined,[120] but the fact of dissension over internal policies in Judah which were viewed as economically oppressive. Both the terminology and the point of view of 6:16 are similar to Isa 10:1-2.

The blame for the perceived social upheaval in Judah is placed directly on those who make policy and administrative decisions. Recognition of this fact explains why the prophet perceived the resulting violation of property rights as rampant and effective: apparently these statutes were enforced with the authority of the state.

Summary and Conclusions

These texts from the eighth century prophets are fragmentary, formulated often in impersonal style, and use traditional forms of speech. They also reflect the views of public spokesmen who perceived a dissolution of society, a crisis in communal relations, the loss of some personal rights concerning private property, and a failure in certain institutions to maintain social equilibrium.

These specific texts were chosen for examination because they represent the references to property rights in the eighth-century prophets. An advantage to this approach is that it allows for cumulative effect. Individual details taken together provide evidence for general conclusions which can be summarized as well as other conclusions which themselves require more elaboration.

Generally speaking, these texts show much overlap in theme despite some variety in terminology. For example, while Amos and Isaiah speak of the poor and needy *(dallīm, ʿanāwīm)*, Micah does not use those terms even though it is relatively certain that he grapples with many of the same social problems with which they dealt. Similarly, Amos never refers to the widows and orphans as does Isaiah and probably Micah (2:9), although it would be unrealistic to suppose the plight of such people was much better in northern Israel than in Judah. One point does emerge from this discussion of the differences in terminology. The language about the care of the poor and needy is often found in conjunction with statements about the process of

---

120   *Supra.*, Introduction.

disenfranchisement and the loss of possessions, and thus demonstrates that the description of the poor as the propertyless[121] proletariat is misleading with regard either to Amos, Micah or Isaiah. Such terminology is used by these prophets for classes of people who are losing their land, movable property and rights of possession, not those who lacked these things.

Another issue arising from this investigation concerns the relationship between these accusations of the prophets, pentateuchal texts related to similar topics, and statutes based on royal decree (Chart One presents these texts in tabular form).[122] As discussed in the introduction, a prominent view among scholars is that the prophets based their accusations on certain laws now incorporated in the Pentateuch. Perusal of Chart One will quickly confirm that most texts cited by scholars as evidence for this general view are found in this list dealing with the more restricted topic of property. The relationship between what is now embedded in the Pentateuch and the statutes enacted by various monarchs in Israel and Judah complicates an already difficult problem in discussing the relationship between the accusations of the prophets and pentateuchal or covenant law.

As a result of historical/critical analysis, scholars in the late nineteenth century had assumed that, apart from the Book of the Covenant in Exod 21-23, the legal *corpora* in the Pentateuch were dated later than the eighth-century prophets.[123] The discussion over chronological priority has continued to be a major part of scholarly debate even though the recent tendency is to date substantial segments of the legal *corpora* to the pre-exilic period, at least in a pre-literary form.[124]

---

[121]   Against H. van Oyen, *Ethik des Alten Testaments* (Gütersloh: Gerd Mohn, 1967) 78; and Hentschke, *Satzung*, 13.

[122]   Chart One has several references to 1 Sam 8:14-16, a passage obviously not in the Pentateuch. It is included in the Chart because Samuel's speech in 8:11-17 presupposes that several of the king's rights were actual practices and had the force of state law behind them.

[123]   Duhm (*Theologie*, 116 and note 1) states Amos may have known Exod 21-23. Wellhausen (*Geschichte*, 110) speaks of the prophets as the founders of the religion of law.

[124]   To contrast with Duhm or Wellhausen, cf. Würthwein ("Amos Studien," 48) where he speaks of Amos proceeding point for point in his accusations with what the law forbids.

Over sixty years ago the sociologist Max Weber attached great importance to the social and ethical development he saw in the legal *corpora* of the Pentateuch (Book of the Covenant, proto-Deuteronomy, Holiness Code). For him the Book of the Covenant presupposed land-owning, village-dwelling peasants (i.e., the basic social structure of Israelite society), and dated to the period of the kings or even earlier. Weber said of Deut 12-26, "seizure and debt right was the genuine area of this social law code also and to an even greater extent than in the Book of the Covenant."[125] The Holiness Code (Lev 17-26) presupposed these two sources and contained theological constructs such as the law of Jubilee which were never enacted. Weber noted that the concerns of the prophets and of the legislators responsible for the legal *corpora* affected each other in their attempts to mediate YHWH's will. The precise dating of the legal *corpora* was secondary to the importance of this mutual relationship and shared concerns. Those scholars who argue for prophetical dependence on the ethical stipulations of the law generally follow this approach--though rarely citing Weber--even though not one pentateuchal quotation occurs in the eighth-century prophets.

There are, however, certain differences in emphasis between the concerns of the eighth-century prophets and those evidenced in the pentateuchal legal *corpora* which are particularly well illustrated by the respective approaches to property rights. to begin with, the reality of indebtedness and resulting slavery were major concerns to the prophets. One gathers from the words of an Amos (8:4) or a Micah (2:9) that, any legislation to the contrary, debt slavery was often permanent. There is nothing in either prophet to suggest their acceptance of this situation or of the stipulations in Exod 21:2-6 and Deut 15:12-14, 18, which mandate a six-year period before the release of a (debt) slave. We have concluded instead that Amos and perhaps Micah as well opposed debt slavery. Their attitude *may* have been more in line with Lev 25:39-42, where an Israelite debtor was to be a hired laborer rather than a slave. In any case, it is obvious from other texts such as Jer 34:8-16[126] and Neh 5:2-5 that (debt) slaves could receive an arbitrary and inconsistent

---

125   Weber, *Judaism*, 61-89. The quotation is from 67-68.

126   N. Sarna, "Zedekiah's Emancipation of Slaves and the Sabbatical Year," *Orient and Occident* (AOAT 22; ed. H. Hoffner, 1973) 143-49, esp. 148 on the relationship between the sabbatical provisions of Deut 15 and Jer 34.

treatment from their owners regardless of the pentateuchal legislation.
The point is that not only do the "laws" and the prophets share concerns
for the rights of debtors, but there seems to be implicit *dis*agreement
over specific measures of treatment for this class of people. Amos and
Micah appear less concerned with the property rights of a creditor or
owner and more concerned with the fate and rights of a debtor. Indeed,
at virtually every point in their preserved writings, the accusations of
the eighth-century prophets assume the rights of debtors, and that the
poor are oppressed with regard to their possessions. While this may be
accounted for because the prophets traditionally represented the rights of
the poor (as opposed to a more "even handed" treatment in the law,
Exod 23:1-3; Lev 19:15), it may also reflect the role of prophecy in
Israelite society. Prophets were often advocates for the underrepresented
and were accusers of those not subject to normal jurisdiction such as
kings and officials.[127] As noted earlier, the relationship between legal
corpora embedded in the pentateuch and royal statutes is quite difficult
to detect. Perhaps if more of the administrative practices of the state
were known, the prophetic accusations would be seen more as criticism
of those policies than anything else that may have been written or
mandated in religious communities.

Both Isaiah (3:12) and Amos (2:8, 5:11) reflect another difference
in their references to various exactions by leading classes of the nation
upon the general populace. 1 Sam 8:14-15 confirms that taxes were
collected on behalf of the king, although the Pentateuch is silent on
such measures. Amos 7:1b and Mic 6:16a are also evidence that royal
statutes and rights involved commercial policies. Similar references are
not found in pentateuchal legislation apart from the reference to royal
trading relations in Deut 17:16. On the other hand, usury was an
exaction that concerned prophet and legislator alike. Overall, however,
the eighth-century prophets appear more concerned about state policies
and rights involving property appropriation than the pentateuchal
compilers.

Another emphasis of the prophets is a concern with the
administration of justice and the system's administrators. While the
pentateuchal sources are not silent on these matters (Exod 18:13-26;
Deut 1:13-17), there are no instructions given for the evaluation or
removal of these officials. In criticizing them, therefore, the prophets

---

[127]   M. J. Buss, "Prophecy in Ancient Israel," *IDBS*, 695-96.

pointed out transgressions where "there was no humanly executed penalty in the system of Israelite society."[128]

These observations have shown that with regard to property rights, there are individual points of divergence and difference between the prophets and the "law." Thus, one cannot use the latter as *the* key to understanding the prophetic accusations concerning property rights. Nevertheless, several of the moral mandates of the pentateuchal corpora may have provided a basis for the prophetic accusations, just as the language of justice and righteous celebrated in the cult likely provided traditional language for the prophets to use.

There are three preliminary conclusions that can be drawn from the preceding analysis of the prophetical texts. (1) It is apparent that something more than the unbridled greed of the wealthy was responsible for the perceived turmoil over property rights. Accusations against state leaders (cf. Chart Two) and various references to exactions suggest that the state itself and its representatives were also responsible. These representatives (officials), however, are not accused of Canaanite practices; to the contrary, what indications are provided clearly imply that the opposed practices are Israelite (or Judaean) and often "legal" though they are consistently judged as unethical. (2) A second conclusion is the recognition that a close relationship exists between the administration of justice and the perceived economic oppression (Amos 2;7a, 5:7, 10, 12; Isa 1;23, 10:1-2; Mic 2:1-2, 3:1). This seems to be a by-product of the first conclusion concerning the negative influence of administrators and officials. Chapters Three and Four will develop this insight further through examinations of different texts. (3) The texts examined imply some basic conflicts between the rights of citizens and those of administrators and officials previously mentioned. A basic conflict in evidence concerns the right to own, possess or sell immovable property, as opposed to the accumulation of such property in the hands of a few. Chapter Two examines this issue in the Hebrew Bible with regard to the property rights and the fourth and fifth chapters examine some sociological and historical reasons for the accumulation of property in the eighth century. A second basic conflict seen in the prophetical texts concerns the right to exact movable property (Amos 2:8, 5:11, 7:1; Isa 3:12, 13-14). Chapter Four examines this issue further and analyzes the rights of certain officials to appropriate goods and produce. Often behind the accumulation of property, whether it be

---

[128]   *Ibid.,* 696

movable or immovable, lay the fact of debt slavery and its bitter effects or the power of the state through its representatives to appropriate.

Chart One

Property Rights in the Prophets with Pentateuchal Texts
Relating to Similar Issues

Prophets	Legal Texts

AMOS:

2:6b,	sale of righteous	Exod 23:8
2:7a,	oppression of poor	Exod 22:20-21; Lev 19:13
		Deut 24:14
2:7a,	perversion of justice	Exod 23:6; Lev 19:15;
		Deut 16:19
2:7b,	copulation with maiden	
	by father and son	Lev 18:15; Exod 21:7-11
2:8a,	pledge violation	Exod 22:25; Deut 24:17
2:8b,	exaction (tax)	1 Sam 8:14-15
3:9-11,	oppression	Exod 22:20-21; Lev 19:13;
		Deut 24:14
5:11,	usury exaction (?)	Exod 22:24; Lev 25:36-37;
		Deut 23:20
5:11,	taxation	1 Sam 8:14-15
7:1b,	taxation	1 Sam 8:14-15

HOSEA:

4:2,	defraud	Lev 5:21-22, 19:11
4:2,	stealing	Exod 20:15
4:2,	adultery	Exod 20:14, Lev 20:10
5:10,	removal of land marker	Deut 19:14, 27:17
7:3,	defraud	Lev 5:21-22, 19:11
12:8-9,	false scales	Lev 19:35-6; Deut 25:13-15

ISAIAH:

3:12,	usury	Exod 22:24
3:12,	taxes	1 Sam 8:14-15
3:14,	depasturing	Exod 22:4
5:8,	coveting	Exod 20:17

| 10:2, | maltreat. widow and orphan | Exod 22:21; Deut 24:17, Deut 27:19 |

MICAH:

2:2,	coveting	Exod 20:17
2:8b,	pledge violation	Exod 22:25
3:10,	no wages (?)	Lev 19:13; Deut 24:15
3:10,	corvée (?)	1 Sam 8:16

Chart Two

National Leaders and the Perversion of Justice

Text	Person/Title	Circumstance

AMOS:

Text	Person/Title	Circumstance
2:7a	---	perversion of justice *(nṭh)*
5:7, 10	(tax collector?)	corruption
5:12	---	bribery, perversion of justice
5:15	---	exhortation for justice in the gate

HOSEA:

Text	Person/Title	Circumstance
12:7	---	exhortation for justice
13:10	judges *(šōpeṭīm)*, officials *(śārīm)*, king	sarcasm over effectiveness

ISAIAH:

Text	Person/Title	Circumstance
1:17	---	exhortation for justice
1:21-28	officials *(śārīm)*, judges *(šōpeṭīm)*, counsellors	thieves, bribery, corruption
3:2	judge *(šōpēṭ)*	removed from the land
3:14	officials *(śārīm)*, elders *(zeqānīm)*	plunder the poor
10:1-2	administrators *(meḥōqēq)*	perversion of justice *(nṭh)*, plunder of widows/orphans
29:21[129]	---	perversion of justice *(nṭh)*

MICAH:

Text	Person/Title	Circumstance
2:1b	---	authority to rob and oppress
3:1,9	heads *(rōʾšīm)*	do not know justice

---

[129]   Possibly later than the eighth century.

	rulers *(qāṣīn)*	
3:11a	heads *(rōʾšīm)*	judge for bribery
7:3	official *(śār)*,	
	judge *(šōpēṭ)*	ask for rewards and bribes

ZEPHANIAH:

3:3[130]	officials *(śārīm)*,	
	judges *(šōpeṭīm)*	act like lions and wolves

---

[130]   Seventh century.

Chapter Two

Land Tenure and Property Rights

The use of the term *nahalāh* (inheritance, property, dwelling place)[1] in Micah 2:2b raises the whole question of land tenure[2] in ancient Israel and more specifically for the subject of property rights, the issue of the sale and exchange of landed property. Land tenure as a property right was evidently a crucial issue in the eighth century. Both Isaiah (5:8) and Micah (2:9) draw attention to the loss of landed property by former owners as examples of social inequity. A primary result of debt slavery was the loss of collateral, so that Amos' bitter remark about the poor of the land coming to an end (8:4) would have the loss of immovable property in mind as well.

The specific issue of immovable property and its sale is one raised by the prophets themselves. The issue of land sale leads to a related issue (or question) concerning the reasons for the prophetic opposition to such endeavors. It is the goal of this chapter to investigate systematically these two related issues against the background of land tenure of the period in general, and particularly with regard to the influential reconstruction proposed by Albrecht Alt for ancient Israel.

---

[1] *KB*, 606-07. Recently G. Gerleman, "Nutzrecht und Wohnrecht," *ZAW* 89 (1977) 313-24, has questioned the translation of *nahalāh* as possessions or inheritance and argued that it usually means dwelling (*Wohnsitz*). In this view he is opposed by the Greek translations which usually render the term by *o klēros* or a cognate. Akkadian, Ugaritic and Phoenician cognates also occur in contexts dealing with inheritance; H. O. Forshey, *The Hebrew Root NHL and its Semitic Cognates* (unpublished dissertation; Harvard University, 1973). Forshey does say, however, that inheritance may be a secondary development of the word from its earlier use in land grants to warriors. In Deut 18:2 it is recorded that the Levites will have no *nahalāh* among their brethren but that YHWH will be their *nahalāh*. Obviously the imagery involved in this text includes both inheritance and possession, and Gerleman's attempts to meet this objection are inadequate.

[2] K. H. Henrey, "Land Tenure in the Old Testament," *PEQ* 86 (1954) 5-15; S. H. Bess, *Systems of Land Tenure in Ancient Israel* (unpublished dissertation, University of Michigan, 1963).

As noted in the Introduction, Alt saw in Mic 2:2b, "a man and his house, a man and his inheritance," an older formula taken over by the prophet that represented the Israelite social ideal. Early Israel was a society of farmers and herdsmen who were intimately related to the soil and cult. These people did not own their own property in the strict sense because YHWH was recognized as the true owner (Lev 25:23). These people were YHWH's *Nutzniesser* in the promised land. Because of this conception of YHWH's real ownership, a family's ancestral heritage was inalienable. Alt's influential words deserve to be quoted in their context.

Um Eigentum im vollen Sinne handelt es sich dabei aber nicht; der Inhaber darf das ihm zustehende Stück Landes nicht beliebig veräussern, verschenken, vertauschen oder verkaufen, sondern nur vererben und kann sich demgemäss fur die Zeit, in der ihm die Bearbeitung obliegt, nur als den verantwortlichen Nutzniesser betrachten: Verantwortlich ist er nicht nur seiner Familie, seiner Gemeinde und seinem Stamm, sondern vor allem dem Gott seines Volkes Jahwe; den dieser ist der eigentliche Eigentümer des ganzen Landes, und ausschliesslich die Verleihung der Anteile durch ihn begründet den beschränkten Rechtsanspruch, den die einzelne Familie, aber auch jede einzelne Familie mit Ausnahme des anders versorgten Stammes Levi auf ihre Ausstattung mit einem bescheidenen erbgebundenen Grundbesitz innerhalf der Ackerflur ihrer Gemeinde erheben kann.[3]

Alt also pointed out that while this system could provide security and stability for family property, there were other factors to be considered about the viability of this system. For example, as families grew and villages expanded new land would be cleared for their use which was probably not always regulated by this older Israelite *Bodenrecht*. Moreover, the inalienability of property limited its use as capital when a family was in debt. If a famine or drought struck, a person holding inalienable property could not easily put it up for capital

---

[3]   Alt, "Der Anteil," 349. Alt cites no texts apart from Mic 2:2b and assumes his reconstruction is generally acknowledged. A footnote to the work of W. Bolle, *Das israelitische Bodenrecht* (theol. diss., Berlin, 1939) suffices for proof.   Bess (Systems, 91) agrees with Alt; "The principle of the inalienability of the land was fundamental to the whole economy of the period of the tribal confederation."

or security. The most important factor to be reckoned with, however, was the different *Bodenrecht* of the indigenous Canaanites who viewed property (land and houses) as simply another form of capital and capable of alienation. Alt saw in the differences between these two systems a basis for understanding much of the conflict witnessed in the prophetic accusations.[4]

Alt's and similar interpretations of the distinctive Israelite *Bodenrecht* have been highly influential in scholarly circles. For example, the importance of Lev 25:23, "the land shall not be sold in perpetuity *(lismitūt),* for the land is mine; for you are strangers and sojourners with me," has been underscored by von Rad as the "Fundament des gesamten altisraelitischen Bodenrecht," and as part of the promise of the land to Israel, it is also understood as a part of the *Leitmotiv* of the entire Hexateuch.[5]   It is possible, however, to acknowledge the importance of these concepts with von Rad without drawing the same conclusions as Alt and others with regard to land tenure and property rights.

In the Hexateuch both tribes and clans are represented as having their own *naḥalāh* in the promised land (Gen 31:14; Num 16:14; Josh 13:7, 14, 23, *et al.*). Most of the references concern the division of land under the direction of Moses and Joshua, and thus represent a theological attempt to understand and provide a basis for settlement patterns. Of the actual management and administration of communal property in ancient Israel, one reads virtually nothing.[6]   Land tenure involves much more the familial control of property with corresponding obligations toward the village/clan. For example, in the case of the

---

4   *Ibid.,* 352-65. Alt uses the evidence from Ugarit and Alalakh for his reconstruction of the Canaanite *Bodenrecht.*   One should be cautious in a comparison of this type. A. F. Rainey, "The Kingdom of Ugarit," *BA* (1965) 105-06, point out that the scribes of Ugarit considered Canaanites to be foreigners!

5   G. von Rad, "The Promised Land and Yahweh's Land in the Hexateuch," *The Problem of the Hexateuch and Other Essays* (New York: McGraw-Hill, 1966) 79-93. This emphasis is elaborated in his *Old Testament Theology,* 1. 296-305.

6   Probably there was some communally held property in Israel. The Levites are described as having something similar to this. Also villages must have controlled some communal grazing territory.

daughters of Zelophahad (Num 27: 1-11, 36:1-12; Josh 17:3-6),[7] it is a question of inheritance*(nahalāh)* for the daughters because Zelophahad died with no sons, the normal heirs of family property. There is also the issue of the obligation to perpetuate Zelophahad's name (cf. Ruth 4:5) within his clan. A subsequent account in Num 36:1-12 involves the tribe of Manasseh in seeking to prevent the loss of Zelophahad's property through exogamous marriage. The decision in both cases illustrates the principle that the ancestral property is to be kept within the extended family or clan as far as the principles of inheritance are concerned. These narratives are also evidence for the fact that efforts to keep such property within these accepted limits were not always successful.

Regardless of Lev 25:23, v 25 of the same chapter recognized that people would have to "sell"[8] their property for financial reasons. Not only is this fact recognized, but also because of the attachment to such property provisions are made for its eventual return to the original owner. (1) The owner can buy it back (Lev 25:26-27). (2) A kinsman may redeem,[9] i.e., pay the price of, the field (Lev 25:25b). (3) In the Jubilee year,[10] except for homes in walled cities, landed property reverted to its original owners (Lev 25:8-12, 29-31). Because the Jubilee year is probably an extension of the sabbatical year (Lev 25:1-8, 25-28), the return to one's family property would seem to be predicated on the annulment of debts associated with the original sale.

The Jubilee legislation of Lev 25 is utopian proposing idealistic measures to improve social conditions. The legislation does not become less utopian if an author actually intended enactment, if attempts were made to enact it, or even if parallels are produced

---

[7]   Source critics make the accounts of Zelophahad's daughters part of the post P editorial work, although Noth observes the accounts are based on older traditions; see his *Numbers* (OTL: Philadelphia: Westminster Press, 1968) 211.

[8]   Lev 25:25. The term sell, *mkr*, may refer to various financial transactions such as foreclosures or fictitious adoption.

[9]   A. R. Johnson, "The Primary Meaning of *G'L,*" *VTSup* 1 (1953) 67-77.

[10]   R. North, *Sociology of the Biblical Jubilee* (AnBib 4; Rome: Pontifical Biblical Institute, 1954).   North thinks the Jubilee year is basically a "bankruptcy law" (p.176).

suggesting it is neither an isolated idea nor necessarily post-exilic.[11] The Jubilee measures are based on the older theological premise that the land is also YHWH's *naḥalāh* (1 Sam 26:19; 2 Sam 14:16; Jer 2:7, 16:18, 50:11; Ps 68:10, 79:1), yet practical means of enforcing compliance with these measures are not even mentioned. Hence the significance of the Jubilee measure lies in the power of its theological premise to persuade and in its witness of the commitment to the integrity of ancestral holdings in the face of land alienation.

The kinsman-redeemer associated with the reclamation of property is known from other biblical sources and evidently was an influence in the preservation of ancestral holdings. For example, in the case of Elimelech's patrimony, Boaz and his unnamed rival are both entitled to the role of redeemer on account of their kinship to the deceased (Ruth 4:3-6). A second case involves the prophet Jeremiah and his purchase of his cousin Hanamel's field (Jer 32:6-12). Jeremiah is approached by Hanamel while in prison and asked to buy the latter's field because, as the prophet is told, "to you is the right *(mišpāṭ)* of possession *(yerūššāh)* and redemption *(geʾūllāh)*." There are other similarities between the case of Boaz and that of Jeremiah; both transactions were officially witnessed and certain conditions were either fulfilled or agreed upon for future enactment. In Boaz's case, the conditions for redemption seem to have included the acquisition of Ruth in marriage[12] and certainly in addition to this, the agreement to meet all of the obligations associated with Elimelech's patrimony.[13] In Jeremiah's case, the deed of sale contained the "term and conditions" (32:11) inherent in the transaction. Both of these cases are important because they illustrate customary law in progress and because they demonstrated the care taken in dealing with family property. Furthermore, both cases

---

[11]   See A. van Selms, "Jubilee Year," *IDBS*, 496-98, who implies that all of these might be true and thus denies that it is utopian. A utopian is simply "one who advocates impractical reforms," *New Standard Dictionary* (New York: Funk & Wagnall, 1961) 2624.

[12]   H. H. Rowley, "The Marriage of Ruth," *The Servant of the Lord and Other Essays* (London: Lutterworth Press, 1952) 161-86: T. & D. Thompson, "Some Legal Problems in the Book of Ruth," *VT* 18 (1968) 79-99.

[13]   Rowley ("Marriage," 175-76) does not take seriously enough the fact that Naomi's property requires redeeming from certain unspecified obligations.

imply that there were often "outside" obligations against the land which had to be met before immovable property could be sold.

The traditional attachment to one's patrimony is clearly seen in the account of Naboth's refusal to sell his *naḥalāh* to Ahab (1 Kings 21:1-19).[14] In the account Naboth is offered either another vineyard or silver in exchange for his vineyard in Jezreel. His explicit refusal is expressed as an oath, "YHWH forbid that I give you the *naḥalāh* of my fathers (21:3)." The oath leaves Ahab so vexed (as the story goes) that Jezebel is forced to rig a jury to condemn Naboth publicly and have him executed on a trumped-up charge.[15] Contrary to the opinions of Alt and others, the account does not necessarily support the view that Naboth's vineyard was inalienable. Nothing is said or alluded to concerning the illegality of the proposed transaction, only of Naboth's abhorrence at the thought of giving up his ancestral property. Neither Naboth nor the narrator cite a statute which would make the proposed sale "illegal."[16] On the other hand, Naboth's refusal is more than an "appeal to filial piety to get out of an awkward situation."[17] His reply to Ahab is at least consistent with the attitude noted elsewhere in the Hebrew Bible that one's patrimony belonged to the family as part of YHWH's blessing. There is no strict prohibition against alienation--even the utopian measures of the Jubilee year recognize the grim fact of

---

[14] For an exhaustive bibliography and thorough study, see R. Bohlen, *Der Fall Nabot* (TTS 35; Trier: Paulinus-Verlag, 1978).

[15] 2 Kings 9:26 speaks of "the blood of Naboth and the blood of his sons," suggesting that they were executed with him (like Achan's family, Josh 2:22-26). The relationship of this verse to 1 Kings 21:1-19 is unclear. For a discussion of Naboth's "crime," see K. W. Whitelam, *The Just King* (JSOTSS 12; Sheffield: JSOT Press, 1979) 174-78. As Whitelam points out, it is probable but not certain that the property of convicted criminals reverted to the crown.

[16] As Bohlen states (*Nabot,* 333) there is no *Rechtssystematik* regarding the land tenure laws in the Hebrew Bible so that detailed conclusions are not always possible. His detailed study of *naḥalāh* and inheritance in the Hebrew Bible leads persuasively to the conclusion that an individual's *naḥalāh* was carefully protected by Israelite *Bodenrecht* even though Naboth's refusal does not imply "die absolute unverausserlichkeit von nahala-Besitz" (349). Moreover, the *nahala-Besitz* was differentiated from other landed property which was more easily alienable.

[17] Against A. Phillips, *Criminal Law,* 151, note 11.

the sale or loss of ancestral property--but there is a consistent testimony in the sources to the view that such alienation of property is ultimately contrary to the well being of the extended family and thus should be avoided. "A house and wealth are the *naḥalāh* (from) fathers (Prov 19:14)."

It is important to stress the wide-ranging implications of the problem of alienation. Stated simply, the question is whether Israelite law would allow the sale of a family's *naḥalāh*-property to a buyer outside its clan or tribe. One's conclusion about this issue directly affects the understanding of the prophetic accusations concerning land appropriation. Alt, who accepted the principle that the early Israelite *Bodenrecht* required inalienability for the ancestral property, further developed a whole theory of dualism in Israel from this conclusion.[18] According to him, Omri bought the hill of Samaria for his new capital as was possible within Canaanite real-estate principles,[19] i.e., Shemer was free to alienate his property. This purchase would not have been possible under Israelite principles. Samaria then became a capital designed to be the Canaanite counterpart to Jezreel and a separate city-state. As Israelite society developed these Canaanite real-estate principles tended to replace *(zu ersetzen)* the older order and the ruling classes in Samaria gained political and economic control outside their original sphere of influence. Thus Alt was able to contrast Naboth's refusal with Shemer's acceptance as illustrative of two different conceptions of *Bodenrecht* and as evidence for a deep-seated dualism in Israel along primarily ethnic lines. The prophetic protest in both kingdoms resulted from the conflict produced between these differing economic systems.

---

[18]   A. Alt, "Der Stadtstaat Samaria," *Kl Sch* III, 258-302, esp. 265-70. Alt's theory has been rejected for good reasons by de Vaux in a review, *RB* 63 (1956) 101-06, and Buccellati (*Cities and Nations*, 181-93). The choice of Samaria was probably little more than an attempt to rival Jerusalem as the King's personal capital and an administrative center.

[19]   *Ibid.*, 264-65. Alt's stress on the influence of Canaanite *Bodenrecht* finds widespread support among many, especially German-speaking scholars. See Bohlen, *Nabot*, 16-18, 343-50, 387-93, for some references. Bohlen himself writes of a *kanaanaischbaalistischer Bodenrechtauffassung* (391) which is part of a *fruhkapitalistische Feudalordnung* (349).

If the possibility of land alienation is accepted in principle under the divided monarchies, even allowing for a conservative family/clan ethic and customary law which sought to restrain the sale of ancestral property, then the large dualism posited by Alt and others[20] is reduced to tensions between competing economic systems within the Israelite *Bodenrecht* itself. As already pointed out, there is no strict prohibition *per se* against land alienation in the Hebrew Bible. Instead various measures are advocated to protect the rights of inheritance with regard to family property. It is much more probable that competing forces and institutions within the larger Israelite society were responsible for the pressures either to use landed property as a convenient form of capital or to preserve its use for the family. Even a Jeremiah, who functioned as a redeemer to preserve a family field, could represent the buying and selling of fields as a sign of YHWH's future blessing (32:15). A socioeconomic structure in which the (extended) family's livelihood is produced on or from its landed property, especially in an agrarian based society such as pre-exilic Israel or Judah, would tend to support the preservation of ancestral holdings within the family. That segment of society which depended on economic specialization and the distribution of agricultural surplus for its livelihood, which would include such people as merchants and government officials, would tend to support the use of land as a form of capital.[21] It is precarious to attribute this latter tendency solely to the Canaanites or to any ethnic segment of

---

[20]   H. Donner, "The Separate States of Israel and Judah," *Israelite and Judaean History* (ed. J. H. Hayes, J. M. Miller; OTL; Philadelphia: Westminster Press, 1977) 399-408, follows the reconstruction of Alt in every respect. The choice of Samaria as another capital shows the Omrides following a "radically dualistic solution of the Canaanite problem" (401). Donner does not say why, based on his reconstruction, Jehu did not reject Samaria for a capital because of its Canaanite jurisdiction.

[21]   For the economic, sociological and anthropological backgrounds for these two conceptions of land and capital, see M. Nash, *Primitive and Peasant Economic Systems*; T. E. Carney, *The Economics of Antiquity*; G. Dalton, ed., *Tribal and Peasant Economics* (Garden City: Natural History Press, 1967): M. Weber, *The Agrarian Sociology of Ancient Civilizations* (London: NLB, 1976). Carney, 15-18, stresses that neither modern capitalistic nor Marxist analysis is adequate or always relevant for these concepts. They are not adequate because the societies were neither western nor industrial, and they become irrelevant for the same reasons.

ancient society. The Canaanites are primarily vilified in the Hebrew Bible for their religious and cultic influence not their economic subversion and influence. This holds true for the prophetic accusations, which do not accuse Canaanite oppressors of replacing Israelite laws, but accuse Israelite oppressors who, when specifically referred to, are often found to be officials who were taking advantage of their positions to further their own gain.[22]

To summarize briefly, there is textual evidence for both a conservative, probably agrarian, viewpoint of land tenure that sought to keep immovable property as a family heritage, and for a more commercially oriented view that assumed the right of ownership included the right of alienation.

There is comparative evidence in other cultures in the ancient Near East for this tension between the preservation of family property and its use as alienable capital. To begin with, the texts discovered at Mari show a flourishing tribal system in existence. Malamat has demonstrated that some of the legal texts employ the term *naḫalum*, a cognate of the Hebrew *nḥl, naḥalāh* which he translates "assign (hereditary) property, apportion."[23] The verb is used, for example, in *ARM* VIII 11, where the Awin clan assigns or apportions some of their property to a certain palace official. To receive the land from the thirteen families of Awin, this official had to go through the "legal fiction" of adoption into the clan.

There are three other transactions involving this same official where the term *naḫalum* is also used (*ARM* VIII 12-14). He is first awarded land from the royal estate of Mari in a *naḫalum* procedure. In two separate payments subsequent to this initial act, he makes two payments back to his benefactor, both of which are also termed termed a

---

[22]   This conclusion is in general agreement with that of Carney (*Economics of Antiquity*, 36) in his comparative approach: "Bureaucracies evolved from the redistributive exchange system and never escaped the influence of their origin. Bureaucracies in antiquity--civil, ecclesiastical and military--were run by the elite. Status distinctions were of the greatest importance---the governmental bureaucracy was regulative and extractive, not developmental."

[23]   A. Malamat, "Mari and the Bible. Some Patterns of Tribal Organizations and Institutions," *JAOS* 82 (1962) 143-50. He follows G. Boyer *Textes Juridiques* (ARM VIII; Paris: Imprimerie Nationale, 1958) 22-29, 166-68, 191-97.

naḫalum procedure. Apparently all three of these transactions were "legal fiction" in the guise of "reciprocal apportioning patrimonies."

The Mari texts demonstrate the need for pseudo-kinship ties and patrimony lines for certain land transactions in order to circumvent opposition to property being sold outside the tribe. Partial reason for this is the fact that the Mari documents reveal at least three types of land tenure:[24] individually owned land, tribally owned and controlled land, and public land owned by the king. As Batto points out, the relationship between the tribal groups and the royal house could be strained by the perceived encroachment of the latter upon land it considered crown property.[25]

Similar circumstances also existed at Nuzi. The texts discovered near Kirkuk provide much information about systems of land tenure and the practices of adoption for legitimacy in the case of property sales.[26] A recent study summarizes the state of research.

> In principle there is a tendency against the sales of immovables outside the circle of family communes--hence derives the use of "adoptions" in order to introduce new people within the family group and let them "inherit" the field. Sales of fields must be considered as transactions concluded because of a state of need: the debtor is compelled to sell his real estate as an ultimate expedient against indebtedness. "Adoptions" in fact represent the final stage of a process which passes through loans with high rates of interest, pledge of relatives or immovables (in most cases the field itself), and definitive transfers of relatives to the creditor. In principle, the price of a field is based upon its rate to produce, but is in fact strongly affected by the unfavourable position of the debtor, who is forced to suffer the pressures of the creditor. As a result, the evaluations of fields are kept to a low level.[27]

---

[24]   B. Batto, "Land Tenure and Women at Mari," *JESHO* 23 (1980) 210-32.

[25]   *Ibid.*, 211, 216.

[26]   Two convenient examples of adoptions are translated in *ANET* 219-20. Detailed studies in H. Lewy, "The Nuzian Feudal System," *Or* 11 (1942) 1-40, 209-50, 297-349; P. M. Purves, "Commentary on Nuzi Real Property in the Light of Recent Studies," *JNES* 4 (1945) 68-86.

[27]   C. Zaccagnini, "The Price of the Fields at Nuzi," *JESHO* 22 (1979) 15.

Zaccagnini had analyzed the sales contracts available from the Nuzi texts before making the assertions just quoted. While similar documents are unfortunately lacking from Israel in the pre-exilic period, his conclusions on the "unfavourable position of the debtor" and the corresponding low price of the fields are interesting to compare with Isaiah's woe speech in 10:1-2. We suggested in the treatment of the passage that a primary intention of the woe speech was to call attention to the unfavorable conditions of a statutory agreement or contract which was perceived as little more than robbery.

At the more commerce-oriented city of Ugarit, the buying and selling of patrimonies was not confined to family members,[28] nor was an adoption clause necessary, although the alphabetic texts do contain many references to the term *nḥl(t)* in the sense of "inheritor." These references appear mainly in the context of a purchaser's heirs regardless of whether he or she were a family member.[29] It has been argued that preference was given to a family member in order that a patrimony might be retained, but the contract cited as evidence *(RS* 17.149)[30] will hardly bear the weight assigned to it. Collective responsibility among rural communities for involvement in local land sales, however, is better documented. Of the more agrarian communities under the political control of Ugarit, some were made up of land-owning families who made many decisions for the whole village and sought to keep control of landed property within the community.[31]

One should not overlook the legislation and discussion associated with the sale of patrimonial property in ancient Greece (800-500 B. C.

---

[28]   G. Boyer, "La place des textes d'Ugarit dans l'histoire de L'ancien droit oriental," in J. Nougayrol, id., *Le palais royal d"Ugarit, III* (Mission de Ras Shamra VI; Paris: Imprimerie Nationale, 1955) 299-305; A. F. Rainey, *The Social Stratification of Ugarit* (unpublished dissertation; Brandeis University, 1962) 31-32, 212-15.

[29]   A. van Selms, *Marriage and Family Life in Ugaritic Literature* (London: Luzac & Company, 1954) 137-43.

[30]   Against M. Heltzer, *The Rural Community in Ancient Ugarit* (Wiesbaden: Ludwig Reichert Verlag, 1976) 100-01. He provides a transliteration of the text.

[31]   *Ibid.,* 90-96.

E.).[32]   Classical scholars are divided over the question of legality in the alienation of the patrimony. The fact is that city-states and their territories differed on their practice of alienation, but there is evidence that at least some regions had customary laws and a conservative, rural ethic which sought to keep patrimonial property within the family.

Reform movements in Greece typically used the slogan, "annulment of debts and redistribution of land."[33]   The slogan is explicit evidence for the close relationship between insolvency and the increasing alienation of family property. There are two other factors that are rather clear about land tenure and reform movements in Greece which allow for some generalization. Both are illuminating for the present study. (1) One's civil rights and obligations were often tied to landownership so that the loss of property meant exclusion from important political processes as well.[34]   (2) The discussion over land tenure in Greek society presupposes what Asheri has called two different patterns.[35]   The first he calls conservative and agrarian and based primarily on independent households and a certain "equality" in land distribution. This pattern favored strict inheritance laws and the inalienability of the family lot. The second pattern, which he calls unprejudiced and liberal, presumes immovables to be of individual ownership in order to promote freedom of business and the accumulation of wealth.

There are several conclusions to be drawn from this brief survey of neighboring cultures with regard to ancient Israel and land tenure. First of all, the provisions in the Hebrew Bible that seek to protect a family's ancestral property reflect a culture and religious ethic which have analogies among these cultures. These provisions are for the most part not unique but presuppose similar socio-economic settings, particularly

---

[32]   D. Asheri, "Laws of Inheritance, Distribution of Land and Political Constitutions in Ancient Greece," *Historia* 12 (1963) 1-21; M. I. Finley, "The Alienability of Land in Ancient Greece," *Eirene* 7 (1968) 25-32; Finley (ed.,) *Problems de la terre en Greece ancienne* (Netherlands: The Hague, 1973).

[33]   M. Austin and P. Vidal-Naquet, *Economic and Social History of Ancient Greece* (Berkeley: University of California Press, 1977) 25, 53-78, 210-12.

[34]   *Ibid.*, 25; Asheri, "Laws," 1-6.

[35]   Asheri, "Laws," 20-21.

with regard to an agrarian context[36] and a close relationship between debts and the sale of immovable property. The principle of inalienation, whether it stems from customary or state law, finds its support among those people whose livelihood depends on the produce of the soil and whose family structure provides the basic means of production. In the Jubilee legislation, it is the landed property which is to revert back to the original owners not the house in a walled city (Lev 25:29-31). Where neither the agrarian structure or family means of production dominates, then immovable property is simply another form of capital (as at Ugarit). In either case, these observations confirm the anthropologist's dictum that, "in most societies land tenure is merely the geographical expression of social structure."[37] Finally, the various patterns of land tenure proposed for Greek society or reconstructed from the Mari texts provide better analogies for pre-exilic Israel and Judah than the reconstruction of Alt and others. Competing social institutions and economic goals within Israelite society *better* account for the conflict over land tenure rights than an ethnic and economic dualism.

There are several prophetic texts which need to be examined in light of these conclusions. To return to the book of Micah, in the exegesis of 2:1-2 it was concluded that the confiscation of a person's property could have some legal justification. The context of the accusations and the terminology employed by the prophet suggest strongly that the confiscation resulted from foreclosure because of insolvency. That such confiscated property could be a family patrimony, a *naḥalāh,* is explicitly stated in 2:2b. These conclusions agree with the view that ancestral property could be alienated from a family on legal grounds for such a reason as indebtedness even though there must have been community pressure to prevent it.

---

36   In the Samaria Ostraca dating to the eighth century B.C.E., one finds in the place and clan names evidence for the agrarian structure of Israelite society and also that these names have parallels in the Manassite clan lists of Num 26:29-34 and Josh 17:1-13, demonstrating that inheritance laws were still at work. See A. Lemaire, *Inscriptions Hebraiques* (LAPO; Paris: Cerf, 1977) 55-65.

37   Nash, *Primitive and Peasant Economic Systems,* 34.

The ironic quotation of Mic 2:4, placed in the mouth of the oppressors, speaks of the "exchange" of property *(yāmīr)*[38] that will result from the approaching disaster. The verb, *mûr*, means exchange in the context of possessions while a cognate noun, *temūrāh*, refers to the exchange itself.[39]   The quotation is ironic because it represents those people as distraught who have confiscated another person's property because they themselves will endure a forced "exchange." Yet the very term employed *(yāmīr)* demonstrates the relative ease of alienating property.

The obscure reference in Mic 2:5 to the casting of lots is difficult to interpret. In the exegesis it was concluded that the reference is to a future redistribution of YHWH's promised land patterned after the canonical version of the first distribution of the land. If this is correct, it links the theological conceptions of property ownership in the Hexateuch with those of the prophet. In the new sacral order the former oppressors will be excluded when the congregation is reconstituted.

Other terminology in the book of Micah supports a basis for the prophet's critique in the sacral traditions about the land as YHWH's blessing to Israel. In the accusation of 2:9, the taking of "delightful" homes from the women and children is described as the taking of YHWH's glory. As pointed out in the exegesis, this term "glory" *(hādār)* and similar terms are used in other contexts with reference to the promised land. Furthermore, the bitter conclusion that the eviction process referred to is permanent *(le'ôlām)* may reflect an awareness that no sabbatical year or kinsman-redeemer will effect reappropriation. In Mic 2:10 the announcement is made that this property acquired through eviction is no place of rest *(menûḥāh).* This term too is used elsewhere in reference to the security of a home (Ruth 1:9) and to the promised land (Deut 12:9; Ps 95:11). The reason that this property is no longer a place of rest is that it is unclean *(ṭom'āh),* a term used in Lev 18:25 to describe the defilement of the land by its pre-Israelite inhabitants (cf. Isa 6:5).

Isaiah's terminology also gives insight into the exercise of property rights. The woe speech of 5:8 implies that the loss of property and

---

[38]   *yāmīr* is the MT reading. It is adopted here by the writer as the preferred reading even though many scholars prefer *yimmād*, "is measured."

[39]   For the verb in the context of land tenure and exchange see Ezek 48:14; for the noun, see Ruth 4:7. ·

homes reduces one's claim to certain other rights given landowning citizens in a community. The harsh statutes of Isa 10:1 probably refer to the obligations associated with the sale of immovables like the stipulations involved in Jeremiah's purchase of Hanamel's field. As Zaccagnini observed, the sale of land is but the final process of getting into debt; the prices were low and the conditions for noncompliance were severe.[40]

There is little in the book of Amos that can be directly linked with the problem of land tenure apart from the prophet's horror that debt slavery will bring the poor of the land to an end (8:4, cf. 2:6-8). Certain references, however, suggest that the prophet, like Micah, knew of some *Landnahme* traditions now embedded in the Hexateuch and their theological claims. The clearest example of this awareness and appropriation for societal critique is found in 2:9-11[41] where, in an extended accusation against Israel, references are made to YHWH who brought them up from Egypt to possess the land of the Amorites (cf. Hos 12:14; Mic 6:4-5). Perhaps the references by the prophet to the cult centers of Bethel, Gilgal and Beer-sheba (4:4, 5:5) are important in this regard. These centers are those associated in the Hexateuch with the promise and occupation of the land, and were certainly centers which preserved Israelite traditions. Amos' critique may reflect his acceptance of the (popular) tradition that YHWH granted the land to the nation, but also that he rejected the social structure and many economic practices in eighth-century Israel. If this is correct, then his demands for socio-economic rectitude are rooted in a demand that YHWH's gift of land and home be morally honored by the recipients.[42]

This discussion of land tenure and property rights can be summarized as follows: (1) The prophetic texts support the conclusion drawn from the discussion of land tenure that the appropriation of land and people results primaril from indebtedness. (2) The sharp critique of property appropriations in the eighth century presupposes customary law designed to protect ancestral property,[43] but cannot be used as

---

40   *Supra.*, note 27.

41   The grounds for denying 2:9-11 to Amos are inadequate; see Rudolph (*Amos*, 145-46).

42   K. Koch, *Die Propheten* (Stuttgart: W. Kolhammer, 1978) 1. 61-62.

43   Bardtke ("Die Latifundien," 247 and note 2) has stated that the strong protest of the eighth-century prophets against land appropriation

evidence for laws of strict inalienability. (3) The specific accusations in the prophetic texts against property appropriation have a theological basis and reflect the view that the customary laws designed to protect family property are also based on Yahwistic traditions about the promise and granting of the land.[44]   It is these traditions which help form the valuation of the land and provide a contrast with the "crimes" of excessive property accumulation. (4) The brief discussion of land tenure shows clearly enough that property rights and laws in ancient Israel do not seem to be unique but have parallels in other cultures where similar socio-economic conditions are found; more specifically, in a primarily agrarian society whose economic base is the landowning family or clan. (5) Neither the texts in the prophets nor those concerned with land tenure provide evidence for the gradual replacement of an Israelite *Bodenrecht* with that based on Canaanite principles. Alt's reconstruction exaggerated the differences in practice between Israelites and the Canaanites, and also attributed too much influence to the latter in the realm of the Israelite economy. One cannot assume homogenous land tenure rights in ancient Israel (or among the Canaanites!). Finally, the prophetic texts presuppose influential Israelites and official institutions such as the judicial system as among the culprits in property appropriation.

---

would be absurd apart from the presupposition of laws concerning the preservation of family property.

[44]   Regarding the assumption of Yahwistic traditions concerning the gift of the land, von Rad (*supra*, note 5) would seem to be correct.

Chapter Three

Property Rights and the Administrative/Judicial System

As indicated in Chapter One, the administrative/judicial system and its administrators received sharp criticism from the eighth-century prophets. The criticism came in large measure from the fact that this system was perceived as a hindrance to the exercise of certain personal and property rights. (Chart Two provides a convenient summary of the evidence for this statement). We have chosen to speak of an administrative/judicial system rather than a judicial court system in recognition of the fact that this system's officials had multiple duties and served differing social institutions.

The purpose of this section is to investigate the relationship between the administrative/judicial system and the prophetic perception of the loss of property rights. First, the relevant material from the prophets is briefly examined. This examination provides a context against which other relevant texts in the Hebrew Bible can be compared and contrasted. The conpleted examination will show that by the eighth century a state administrative/judicial system, with royally appointed officials as its administrators, had developed which overshadowed and overlay the authority of the traditional administrative system (the local assembly of elders). This development was very probably a primary contribution to the conflict over property rights in that century.

Prophets

The demand of the eighth-century prophets for justice *(mišpāṭ)* and righteousness *(ṣedāqāh)* is a *Leitmotiv* of the period. For the present study, their demands have a specific significance as a call for fair-minded officials and honest judges who would properly fulfill their role with regard to property rights. There are, of course, other significant aspects to their demands.

Amos' outcry in 5:7, 10-12 is directed against those who would subvert justice/righteousness. In vs 10 and 12, Amos condemns the unjustness of proceedings in the gate *(ša'ar)*, the place where the administrative/judicial affairs of a community were carried out.[1] Verse 10 refers also to an advocate *(môkîaḥ)* who was evidently a person who argued a case before an assembled group in the gate (cf. Isa 29:21).[2]   Similar themes are sounded elsewhere in the prophet's exhortations' "establish justice in the gate," and "let justice roll down like waters and righteousness like an everflowing stream" (5:15, 24).

All other prophets of the eighth century employed similar exhortations in their demand for *mišpāṭ/ṣedāqāh*.[3]   Isaiah exhorted the people to "establish justice" (1:17) as did Hosea (12:7). Although not an exhortation, Mic 3:1 contains a bitter recognition that the heads of state did not know (practice) justice.

These texts confirm that the eighth-century prophets were concerned with the right ordering of society (or the lack thereof) and its function of mediating YHWH's will. The call for justice presupposes a common understanding between prophet and audience--the call for justice is a demand not an explanation--as well as the sharing of some similar ethical traditions among the prophets themselves.

There is explicit evidence that this concern for justice is directly linked to failures in the administrative system, which in turn is directly related to property rights. This relationship can be stated another way: The concern for justice/righteousness often comes to expression in accusations over the loss of property rights where the context and terminology presuppose a contributing role for the administrative system. An example is Amos' accusation against those who "turn aside *(nṭh)* the way of the humble," in parallelism with those who trample the poor (2:7a). In the context of violated property rights (2:6b-8), the "turning aside" links the administrative/judicial system with the acts of debt slavery, the loss of property used as security, and forced exactions. The verb *nṭh* is used elsewhere to signify the denial of due process and personal rights.[4]   In the context of harassment and bribery, Amos again speaks of those who "turn aside the poor in the gate" (5:12), implying that a cause is perverted at the point of legal or administrative redress. The woe speech of Isa 10:1-2 is another example. In this

---

[1]   Köhler, "Justice in the Gate," 127-50.

[2]   Boecker, *Redeformen des Rechtslebens*, 45-47.

[3]   For the prophetic exhortation see G. Warmuth, *Das Mahnwort* (BET 1; Frankfurt: Peter Lang, 1976).

[4]   Further uses of the word *nṭh* in an administrative/judicial setting are Isa 29:21; Exod 23:6; Deut 16:19; 1 Sam 8:3.

passage the evil statutes and their authors lead to the "perversion of justice for the poor" *(lehaṭṭôt middîn dallîm)*.

Isaiah 10:1-2 is important in this discussion for two reasons. (1) As already stated, the passage is evidence for the effectiveness of the administrative/judicial system and its procedures in depriving the "poor" of what the prophet considered as their rights. They are being plundered and robbed by statute. (2) The persons responsible for making such statutory decisions and administering them acted on the authority of the given statutes; in short, while these persons were probably not lawmakers they acted on the authority of the given statutes and not (just?) as private citizens. Moreover, these persons are not accused of callousness in their administrative duties by allowing the "poor" to be robbed of their property by others, but of taking advantage of their positions to plunder the helpless for their own personal gain.[5]

The references to evil statutes and oppressive writings in Isa 10:1 points to harsh conditions imposed on segments of the population. As such, these conditions would require at least the tolerance and probably the support of the state for authority. Micah 6:16 and its reference to statutes *(ḥūqqôt)* comes to mind in this context where Judah's royal policy is compared to that of the Omrides. These two references provide evidence that Judah of the eighth century had economic practices that were unpopular(at least with Micah and Isaiah), that were deceptive in appropriating property, but seemingly had support in official circles.

For the northern kingdom there is nothing as explicit as Mic 6:16 in either Amos or Hosea. Amos 7:1b is probably an exception, but the statement of the prophet is not given in the form of an accusation nor is the practice of the king's mowings explicitly termed a statute. Similarly, Amos 5:11a is an accusation about exactions but these forced payments are not named as statutes either. In the final analysis, however, both practices (5:11a, 7:1b) would have been part of the administrative system that required the sanction of the state. Exactions and mowings, both of which were probably taxes, must have been regulated by the state and collected for its benefit. One is justified in seeing them as practices based on state regulations if not statutes.

---

5   In speaking of an office or position, it should be noted that biblical Hebrew does not have a word for "office." Instead various functions in ancient Israel were fulfilled by people chosen or appointed to perform them; M. Noth, "Office and Vocation in the Old Testament," in his *The Laws in the Pentateuch and Other Studies* (Philadelphia: Fortress Press, 1967) 229.

The role of the state (royal authority) in the administrative/judicial system can be seen also from the titles of the officials named in the prophetic accusations (cf. Chart Two). Amos' accusations often do not specifically identify those he criticizes even though the context and other references in the book leave little doubt that the inhabitants of Samaria and their influence are primarily in view. An often overlooked reference in Hosea, however, provides a contemporary comment on the general administrative system in Israel (13:10).

Where now is your king that he may save you from all your enemies, and your judges (šōpeṭīm) of whom you said, give me a king and officials *(šārīm)?*[6]

This sarcastic question is one of several texts in Hosea which contain a radical critique of kingship.[7]   The text is important because it recognizes the necessary relationship between a monarch and his officials; with the monarch come the administrators of royal policy and their corresponding privileges. The administrative/judicial role of these officials is clear from the references to them as judges and officials, and the military overtones of their positions are not absent either. Hosea's sarcasm provides two important pieces of information. (1) There were officials in the northern kingdom of the eighth century who had the title and duties of judge. (2) These officials were closely related to royal policy.   This second point is a logical conclusion from Amos' prophecies against Samaria's inhabitants and the nature of his accusations, but that some of the persons were called judges or officials could not be demonstrated from the texts.

Similar circumstances can be demonstrated for Judah.   In a depiction of Jerusalem (1:21-26), the city's officials *(šārīm)* are described as thieves and men who pursue bribes rather than those who would adjudicate fairly *(špṭ)*. A *šōpēṭ* is included in the notables that YHWH is removing from the land (3:2).   Further correspondence between the concept of *mišpāṭ/špṭ* and officials responsible for the

---

[6]   Reading   *ʾayyēh* for *ʾehī* of MT with virtually all commentators, and *ṣārekā* for *ʿārekā*; cf. J. Mays, *Hosea*, (OTL; Philadelphia: Westminster Press, 1969) 176; the more extensive reconstructions offered by Wolff (*Hosea*, 221) are not convincing.

[7]   A. Gelston, "Kingship in the book of Hosea,"*OTS* 19 (1974) 71-95; and F. Crüsemann, *Der Widerstand*, 85-94.

violation of property rights is found in Isa 3:13-15 and 10:1-2. In the former passage, the śārîm and zeqānîm have taken advantage of their position to rob their fellow citizens. The śārîm are usually of royal blood or appointment and the "elders" are male family and clan heads with various responsibilities. Whether the specific title of "judge" is also applicable to them or the unnamed officials in 10:1 is unknown.

Micah's vocabulary is further confirmation that the title of judge existed at this time (7:3), although the function of adjudication and rule inherent in the title was also performed by the rō'šîm and qāṣîn of 3:1. Micah 3:11a states that Zion's rō'šîm judge for a price and the priests instruct for the same. This accusation confirms that "judging" was not just an office but a function performed by various persons of differing rank or title. Such people are called Zion's "heads" but this seems to refer to their source of authority not the geographical limitation of their influence. Whether the instruction of the priests refers to the realm of civil administration is not certain.[8]

Evidence from these texts can be summarized in the following manner. (1) The administrative/judicial system played a prominent role in the prophetic accusations because it did not protect the property rights of certain people (Amos 5:7, 10, 12; Isa 1:23, 10:1-2; Mic 2:1-2, 3:1-4, 11). The gate of a city as well as the capital cities were the places that witnessed, regulated and processed such cases as debt slavery, property sales, foreclosure, the collection of taxes, etc. These transactions and their institutional setting were part of a system which was perceived as contributing to the problem of injustice rather than functioning as an adequate check or balance. (2) There were various

_____

[8]   According to Deut 17:10, the levitical priests and the judge (in Jerusalem) shall instruct (yrh) in difficult cases brought to them. This is the same verb used in Micah 3:11. The precise jurisdiction of the priests in 17:10 is unclear. Perhaps they were concerned only with sacral and cultic matters, or with matters that required an answer by lot from YHWH, or their duties extended to all difficult cases. B. Mazar, "The Cities of the Priests and Levites," VTSup 7 (1960) 193-205, contends that the priests and levites had a role in royal administrative policy in border areas. He draws on texts whose date and reliability are uncertain so that it is difficult to make historical judgments. There may be an indication of a priest with royal administrative duties in Amos 7:10-17. The fact that Amos was opposed by Amaziah the priest at Bethel, when his preaching had emphasized social crimes rather than cultic sins, could mean that Amaziah's duties as a royal appointee extended beyond regular cultic duties.

officials responsible for the perceived failure of this system and who benefited from its perversion. These officials were closely related to the monarchy and apparently were participants in the administration of state affairs (Hos 13:10; Isa 1;21-26; Mic 3:1). Some also implemented unpopular regulations (Amos 5:11; Isa 10:1-2) which were partially responsible for the prophetic outcry.

Pentateuchal and Historical Texts

These two summary observations (above) highlight issues which require scrutiny of other texts in the Hebrew Bible. One institution requiring critical examination is the administrative/judicial system. The task is not to make an exhaustive history of research but to ascertain, when possible, significant features and developments against which to understand the prophetic texts. Some general observations are made which are followed by a more detailed examination of certain pentateuchal and historical texts.

The primary administrative institution in premonarchical Israel was the assembly of elders--heads of families, clans and property owners--who represented their kin and cities when making decisions. In the absence of a state government and kingship, this administrative institution was a primary and basic force in local affairs. These assemblies met at the gate of the city when circumstances warranted in order to conduct local affairs, usually meeting early in the morning before members would depart for the fields. It was not always necessary to make a decision or judgment but only to serve as witnesses.[9] Property sales are a good illustration of this reconstruction. Both Abraham and Boaz are recorded as purchasing land in the presence of elders in the gate who both confirm and witness the proceedings (Gen 23:10-18; Ruth 4;1-11).

Premonarchical Israel may have possibly possessed officers and judges who exercised more than local judicial authority (adjudication in a local setting would have been the function of either the assembled group of elders or specific persons among them with acknowledged authority). Some centralized authority was necessary for military

---

[9]   D. McKenzie, "Judicial Procedure at the town gate," *VT* 14 (1964) 100-04.   For the premonarchical period, see J. D. Salmon, *Judicial Authority in Early Israel* (Princeton; unpublished dissertation, Princeton Theological Seminary, 1968).

strategy, but the question of a centralized administrative/judicial system remains open. It has been suggested that early Israel formed a sacral confederation of tribes with judges who proclaimed and interpreted the divine law at a central sanctuary.[10]   According to Noth, the judge(s) of the confederation or amphictyony were a pattern for the later office of a central judge (Deut 17:8-13; Mic 4:14); and the distinctive laws and Yahwistic customs of the confederation were a source of opposition in pre-exilic Israel to the corrupting influence of the "Canaanite ethos."[11] This influential reconstruction of an early Israelite amphictyony has been increasingly rejected,[12] casting doubt on the existence of any central legal institution in the premonarchical period. The two lists of minor judges (Judg 10:1-5, 12:7-15), on which Noth based much of his argumentation, simply do not provide enough evidence for a *central* office. The circuit-court of Samuel (1 Sam 7:16) is evidence for the judicial authority of an individual that included more than a single town, but the cities mentioned in the text (Bethel, Gilgal, Mizpah) are located too close together to be representative of an all-Israel judicial system.

The references cited above from the book of Judges represent some of the textual evidence for premonarchical leaders in early Israel called judges. Examination of the semantic range of *špṭ*, however, shows that the word has a wider connotation than just a juridical or forensic meaning.[13]   This range of meaning is important for defining these early leaders as well as understanding the subject of administrative practice. Several passages where either the verb or noun *(šōpeṭīm, mišpāṭ)* is used have the sense of "rule" or "govern" in addition to the juridical meaning. Whitelam has conveniently collected some of these

---

[10]   M. Noth, *Das System der Zwölf Stämme Israels* (BZWANT 4/1; Stuttgart: Kolhammer Verlag, 1930); *Ibid.*, "Das Amt des "Richters Israels'," *Gesammelte Studien zum Alten Testament* (TBU 39; Münich: Chr. Kaiser, 1969) 1. 71-85.

[11]   M. Noth, "The Laws in the Pentateuch," *Laws*, 29 and footnote 64.

[12]   For a balanced discussion and bibliography, O. Bächli, *Amphiktyonie im Alten Testament* (TZ 5; Basel: Friedrich Reinhardt, 1977).

[13]   W. Richter, "Zu den 'Richtern Israels'," *ZAW* 77 (1965) 40-72; K. W. Whitelam, *The Just King* (Sheffield: JSOT Press, 1979) 51-61.

passages[14] where the word is: (1) associated with *šār* (Exod 2:14; Amos 2:3; Mic 7:3; Zeph 3:3; Prov 8:16), (2) associated with *mlk* (Hos 7:7; Ps 2:10), (3) associated with both *mlk* and *šār* (Hos 13:10; Ps 148:11), (4) associated with other ruling and governing titles (Isa 33:22, 40:23; 2 Chron 1:2). Perhaps the best link between the various functions of judge/rule/govern inherent in *špṭ* is demonstrated in the request to Samuel for a king "to judge us," where the verb is used three times (1 Sam 8:5, 6, 20). Cognate languages provide additional support for this semantic range and function of the word.[15]

1 Sam 8:20 is evidence also for the close relationship between ruling a people *(špṭ)* and military leadership. This relationship seems to be the key in understanding the role of the leaders in early Israel. A person who "judged Israel" was often a leader who organized tribal leagues or groups for defense.[16] This military connotation to ruling a people remained important with the advent of kingship and, as 1 Sam 8:11-17 assumes, it became the basis for a newly emerging social structure under statehood.

Between the premonarchical era and the period treated by the eighth-century prophets, the most significant sociological development was the institution of kingship. The king had an important role in the judicial system although his precise function is still disputed.[17] Along with kingship came the practice of royally appointed officials. Various texts in Deuteronomy show that the earlier practice of local elders assembling in the gate existed throughout the pre-exilic period along with developments under kingship (Deut 19:12; 21:2, 4, 6, 19, 22:15, 18, 25: 7). The local assembly of a city, therefore, provided some continuity in the administrative realm of the change from tribal rule to state government. Other passages, however, suggest that with kingship came royal appointments of regional officials that led to a significant reduction in authority for the local administrative/judicial

---

14   Whitelam, *Just King*, 52.
15   *Ibid.*, 55-59.
16   T. Ishida, "The Leaders of the Tribal Leagues 'Israel'," *RB* 80 (1973) 514-30.
17   Two scholars who have recently treated this subject are G. Macholz, "Die Stellung des Königs in der israelitischen Gerichtsverfassung," *ZAW* 84 (1972) 157-82; *ibid.*, "Zur Geschichte der Justizorganization in Juda," *ZAW* 84 (1972) 314-40; and Whitelam, *Just King.*

system (Exod 18:13-27; Num 11:16-17, 26-30; Deut 1;9-17, 16:18, 17:8-13; 2 Chron 19:5-11). According to these passages in the Pentateuch, the judicial affairs of the nation were so burdensome on Moses that judges were appointed to ease the administrative load. The single passage from 2 Chronicles make Jehoshaphat of Judah the author of a substantial reorganization in the administrative sphere that has enough similarities to Deut 1:9-17, 16:18, 17:8-13 to suggest the passage is in part a later, post-exilic account developed from the organization described in Deuteronomy.[18] Jehoshaphat's reform is an aid to understanding the development of the judicial system in Judah but it cannot be treated in isolation from the pentateuchal accounts of Mosaic reorganization. The assumption of many scholars--including the present writer--is that even though older traditions may well have been incorporated into the various accounts, they reflect the age of their composition as well, and provide information on later practices and ideas. The theological presupposition of the Pentateuch's compilers is that law and instruction were mediated to Israel through Moses; the fact is that subsequent developments in legal and cultic practices are habitually retrojected back to Sinai. It is difficult, however, to assign these specific pentateuchal accounts with any confidence to the generally recognized sources J, E, D, and P. It is sufficient to note that they are related in theme and yet derived from earlier, distinct traditions[19] (see Chart Three for a tabular account of the various

---

18   J. Wellhausen, *Prolegomena to the History of Israel* (New York: Meridian, 1957) 191, believes the account in 2 Chronicles is ascribed to Jehoshaphat for etiological reasons; the king's name means "YHWH judges." E. Junge, *Der Wiederaufbau des Heerwesens des Reiches Juda unter Josia* (BWANT 75; Stuttgart: Kolhammer Verlag, 1937) 81-93, thinks the account is a later reflection on the Josianic reform.

19   The passages in the book of Deuteronomy are obviously assigned to the Dtr/DtrH. The difficulty over the source designations for Exod 18:13-27 and Num 11:16-17, 24-30 can easily be seen by comparing commentaries. For example, G. B. Gray, *Numbers* (ICC; New York: Charles Scribner's Sons, (1963) 111, 116, admits the difficulty of source analysis in comparing these two accounts and finally assigns both to E! J. Plöger, *Literarkritische, Formgeschichtliche und Stilkritische Untersuchung zum Deuteronomium* (BBB 26; Bonn: Peter Hanstein, 1967) 31, argues the differences in the accounts of Deut 1:9-18, Exod 18:13-27 and Num 11:16-17, 24-30 make the Deuteronomistic passage independently formulated but dependent on an earlier source or tradition that is nevertheless different from the other two canonical accounts!

passages). Exod 18:13-27, the first account according to the canonical order, may also preserve some of the oldest traditions and will be analyzed first. The other passages are examined in turn, Numbers, Deuteronomy, and 2 Chronicles.

Exodus 18:13-27

Chapter 18 is well known because of its narration of the relationship between the Israelites and the Kenites as personified by Moses and Jethro. The second half of the chapter is devoted to the implementation by Moses of a new administrative/judicial system on the advice of Jethro whereby certain men from the people were selected to help Moses judge they many people who needed his instruction. Scholars have long recognized that this system must have approximated actual practice at some point in Israel's history.[20] Knierim has concluded that the account is an etiology providing a Mosaic warrant for the action of the Judaean king Jehoshaphat, whose judicial reorganization is narrated in 2 Chron 19:4-11.[21] Noth, on the other hand, cautiously suggested that some older elements from Israel's past were preserved because of the friendly relations assumed between Midian and Israel along with the startling idea that Moses needed the advice of a Midianite priest.[22] In all probability the narrative was not solely conceived for an etiological purpose,[23] yet it does reflect an attempt to invest the appointment of regional judges and officials with Mosaic authority in order to form a basis for later, monarchical practice.

There is a certain tension in the account between the sacral obligation of the Mosaic office to inquire of God (v 15b, 16) and the very general description of the administrative duties assigned to the local appointees (v 22). Not enough evidence exists, however, to make a distinction between sacred and profane duties among the respective offices.[24]

---

[20] M. Noth, *Exodus* (OTL; Philadelphia: Westminster Press, 1962) 150.

[21] R. Knierim, "Exodus 18 und die Neuordnung der mosaischen Gerichtsbarkeit," *ZAW* 73 (1961) 146-71.

[22] Noth, *Exodus*, 150.

[23] In agreement with B. Childs, *The Book of Exodus* (OTL; Philadelphia: Westminster Press, 1974) 329-32.

[24] As Noth (*Exodus*, 150) would like to propose.

The only differentiation made in the account is between large (gādōl) and small (qāṭōn) cases, with the former being referred to Moses by the local courts. No criteria for distinguishing between these two types is given; presumably the local courts decided what was referred to "Moses" (v 26), but the account is silent on this matter.

An important point concerns the men appointed as judges. In addition to the moral qualifications, the placing of men as officials (śārīm) over thousands, hundreds, fifties and tens is a clear reflection of the hierarchy of military organization.[25] This is very important in that it suggests an overlap between the military organization with its leaders and the administrative/judicial system of the nation with its officials.[26] Equally as important as the shared leadership of these two social institutions is the fact that the resulting social structure is based more on 'state' appointment than traditional clan/village loyalties. Knierim rejected the force of this conclusion as valid for the original E account; in his opinion the references to the military levy in vs 21b, 25b are secondary and date from the time of Josiah when the administrative system and the military organization of Judaean citizenry were largely identical.[27] His conclusions on this point are unsatisfactory. For example, he questions whether the rōʾšīm can be identified with the śārīm--and ignores such a text as Deut 20:9b where the relationship between the two terms in a military context is obvious. There is no reason why such a relationship must have developed in the reign of Josiah. It is better with Noth[28] to accept not only the unity of vs 13-27 but also with this conclusion the implications of the

---

25   1 Sam 8:12, 22:7, 29:2; 2 Sam 18:1; Isa 3:3; 2 Kings 1:9; Num 31:14, 48, 52, 54. Gottwald (*The Tribes of Yahweh*, 269-78) argues that premonarchical Israel had a military levy with an ʾelep unit. We believe that Exod 18:13-27 reflects monarchical military organization, regardless of the merits of Gottwald's suggestion in some other contexts.

26   See Chapter Three, Excursus One, on this same phenomena in the Yavneh Yam Letter.

27   Knierim, "Neuordnung," 155, 168-71; Lemaire, *Inscriptions Hebraiques*, 262.

28   Noth, *Exodus*, 146.

account that the leadership of the military organization and of state administration were closely related.[29]

The central thrust of Exod 18:13-27 is to provide a basis for the appointment of local judges--although only the verb *špṭ* (v 22) is used and not the specific title--and also to establish a working, hierarchical relationship between these local appointees and the central authority. The sociological implications of the a passage are more important than assigning it a precise date; however, the mid-ninth century is reasonable in the latter regard. One has only to substitute a monarch for "Moses" to see how the system worked under kingship.[30]

Numbers 11:16-17, 24-30

This passage(s) presents the lifting of Moses' administrative burden by the appointment of seventy elders who receive the "spirit" and the gift of prophecy. It is an anomaly in comparison to the other accounts. Apart from the context of Moses' troublesome load and the administrative employment of elders and officers *(šōṭerīm)*, the emphasis on ecstatic prophecy overshadows the administrative change. No institution of seventy elders is known in Israel until the second temple period except for the obscure reference to a group of elders in Exod 24:1-11 who accompany Moses and others up Mt. Sinai. Secondly, no instructions are given with regard to administrative procedure, judicial practice or ethical requirements. Some scholars, therefore, have suggested that Num 11 is a merging of two separate and earlier accounts. Gray, for example, thinks v 17b is a later addition designed to link an account of seventy elders who prophesy with another account of the people burdening Moses with demands for meat. Taken together these accounts make up the canonical narrative which seems similar in nature to Exod 18:13-27.[31] By this reckoning the relative clause in v 16a--the reference to elders and officers--must be an

---

[29]   Knierim's point about the secondary nature of vs 21b, 25b, is odd because he recognizes that the military organization was usually related to and used by the *state* administration (167-68).

[30]   Some other depictions of Moses in the Pentateuch may be based on later kings; see J. R. Porter, *Moses and Monarchy* (Oxford: Basil Blackwell, 1963). Porter does not connect Exod 18:13-27 with monarchical practice.

[31]   Gray, *Numbers*, 111-12.

addition too because it supports the view that the seventy are chosen for their administrative value.[32]

It is correct to see in Num 11 a merging of two earlier traditions; but one tradition containing vs 16-17 (in their entirety), 24-30 about the continuation of Moses' prophetic office and another concerning meat in the wilderness. That means the tradition about Moses' burden (maśśā᾽) was integral to both earlier accounts (cf. vs 11, 17) and they have merged because the catchword "burden" is shared.

Nothing further is made of the fact that a collegium of elders is to share administrative duties and the spirit of prophecy with Moses, either in Numbers or elsewhere in the Hebrew Bible. The account in chapter 11 *possibly* has links to the practice of prophecy for pay mentioned in 1 Sam 9:8-10; Mic 3:5, 11; Jer 8:10b-11. For authority and material gain, some prophets may have claimed continuity with Mosaic instruction. In all its obscurity, the account does argue for continuity from Moses to his administrative successors and this is a pattern found elsewhere in the Pentateuch.

Deuteronomy 1:9-18, 16:18-20, 17:8-13

The provisions for an administrative/judicial system in Deuteronomy give information supplementary (and contradictory) to the account in Exod 18:13-27. Indeed, the administrative/judicial system presupposed by the book of Deuteronomy is difficult to reconstruct. On the one hand, information is given about the local and central courts with their officials; and on the other hand, the local elders have administrative/judicial functions to perform as well (19:12, 21:2, 4, 6, 22:15, 18). These different guidelines for processing judicial problems can only be partially explained on the supposition of separate functions. They are probably evidence for the imposition of a state appointed and directed system on another system of locally administered judicial practices.

The seeming confusion over administrative detail is illustrated by the case concerning action to be taken after the discovery of a corpse (21:1-9), where the elders and judges act together to measure the distance from the corpse to the closest cities. Subsequent acts are performed by the elders alone making the only reference to judges (v 2)

---

32   That the relative clause in v 16a is an addition is the opinion of M. Noth, *Numbers* (OTL; Philadelphia: Westminster Press, 1966) 87.

seem awkward. Verse 5 contains another awkward reference to the levitical priest that interrupts the instructions for the ritual expiation process and is probably a secondary expansion. This one example illustrates the nature of the deuteronomistic presentation where, as von Rad proposed, different traditions are interwoven.[33]

Deut 1:9-18 rehearses part of the Sinai (Horeb) experience. Parts of the Num 11 tradition and that of Exod 18:13-27 seem presupposed, but the differences in detail make the literary relationship almost impossible to determine.[34] There is agreement in each case, however, that an administrative change was effected under the direction of Moses. The closest points of agreement exist between Exod 18:13-27 and this passage. The moral qualifications are described differently (cf. Exod 18:21a; Deut 1;13), but the leaders are described as $rō'šīm$ over the people in both accounts and most strikingly of all, as $śārīm$ of thousands, hundreds, fifties and tens.[35] The reference to the $šōṭerīm$ in Deut 1:15 finds a parallel in Num 11:16, 2 Chron 19:11 and Deut 16:18, but is lacking in the Exodus account. These $šōṭerīm$ probably assisted judges and were involved in the military levy as well (cf. Deut 16:18, 20:5, 8, 9).[36]

The sequence of 1:9-18 is misleading because it seems to separate the functions of the leaders and the judges, and thus suggests two different groups of appointees. The requirements of 1:13 list traits that by definition include judicial skills and surely are to be related to the burdens and strife of v 12. It is true that judges are mentioned for the first time in v 16, but this reference is not the beginning of a new topic but a series of instructions to the newly appointed leaders (now called judges) of v 15 who were taken and installed by Moses.[37] Otherwise, if v 16 is not a series of instructions for the new leaders/judges, then

---

[33]   So G. von Rad, *Deuteronomy* (OTL; Philadelphia: Westminster Press, 1966) 136.

[34]   *Supra.*, note 19.

[35]   Exodus 18:21, 25 and Deut 1:15 are the only places in the Hebrew Bible where this full pattern of numbered groupings are found.

[36]   J. van der Ploeg, "Les soterim d'Israel," *OTS* 10 (1954) 185-96, concludes that these officers developed under the monarchy and had similar functions to those of the modern police, being involved as assistants to judges, officers in the army, and corvée leaders.

[37]   Against von Rad (*Deuteronomy*, 40) who thinks the judicial and military functions are divided between different persons.

the passage would present the anomaly of instructions to judges whose appointment is not narrated and also the appointment of administrators whose instructions are missing.[38]   This passage, therefore, is in agreement with Exod 18:13-27 in suggesting that the leadership for the military levy and the state administrative/judicial system shared common personnel. While the leaders *may* be considered professionals because of their appointment, those led or grouped in ranks are probably not professional soldiers but citizens organized through a periodic census.

Deut 16:18 urges the appointment of *šōpeṭīm* and *šōṭerīm* in local towns by the citizens. The "democratic" nature of this appointment seems more apparent than real.[39]   First of all, the *šōṭerīm* are almost always officials whose authority rested on the state and not a local appointment. Second, parallel passages (Exod 18:13-27; Deut 1:15) state explicitly that such persons as local judges were state appointed[40] One cannot deny, however, that some form of local nomination or at least acknowledgment is envisioned for the selection process. Indeed, the responsibility assigned to local citizens may reflect a reform in the process of judge selection whereby the control formerly exercised by the central authority ("Moses" or the king) is being shared.

Deut 17:8-13 deals with an appeals court-system for the nation that is presupposed by the other accounts of Moses' administrative reorganization at Sinai. Various difficult cases are referred (by the local judges?) to the higher court consisting not of "Moses" but of levitical priests and a judge(s). Differing opinions have been offered on the interpretation of this passage, some suggesting that only the priests[41]

---

38   For other passages concerning the administrative/judicial system having instructions or lists of qualifications for their officials, see Exod 18:21a, 23:1-3, 6-9; Deut 16:19-20; 2 Chron 19:6-7. Perhaps the exhortations of the prophets for justice in administrative dealings are derived from such material where a recognized ethical tradition is perceived as flouted.

39   Cf. Deut 1:13-14, where the people are asked to choose leaders, with Deut 1:15, where Moses takes and installs them.

40   Both von Rad (*Deuteronomy*, 114) and A. D. H. Mayes, *Deuteronomy* (New Century Bible; London: Oliphants, 1979) 264, think the judges named reflect a state appointment system during the monarchical period.

41   Mayes, *Deuteronomy*, 268-69; G. Seitz, *Redaktionsgeschichtliche Studien zum Deuteronomium* (BWANT 93;

are original to the passage, only the judge(s),[42] or that both belong.[43] One can argue any of the positions; however, the movement toward religious and political centralization which the book of Deuteronomy supports would require a central court that was capable of dealing with any problem arising from a local dispute. Both priests and judges would be needed for the appropriate ruling.

Finally, the penalty for non-compliance with the central court is death. This expressed penalty is indicative of the court's authority and its ability to influence the outcome of local cases.

2 Chronicles 19:4-11

The Chronicler reports that part of Jehoshaphat's reforming activity[44] included a judicial reorganization. He placed judges in the fortified cities (cf. 2 Chron 17:2) instructing them that they judge for YHWH and not for man. Also, he established a central court in Jerusalem comprised of priests, levites and heads of families that ruled on cases referred to it from their brethren. This central court had the services of other levites as šōṭerīm.

There are problems involved in asserting a historical basis for this account. It has no parallel in 1 Kings making the account in the post-exilic book of Chronicles the only explicit claim for a purported mid-ninth century organizational reform. Furthermore, some of the roles of the officials (e. g., chief priest, levites) appear post-exilic. Wellhausen concluded that the account was an etiology based on Jehoshaphat's name, and most scholars have agreed that Deut 16:18, 17:8-13 have influenced the depiction of the court system.[45]

Stuttgart: W. Kolhammer, 1971) 200-202, esp. 202 and note 316. The latter scholar surveys earlier opinions on the question.

[42] Von Rad, *Deuteronomy*, 118. More than one judge is suggested by the plural reference in 19:17.

[43] M. Weinfeld, *Deuteronomy and the Deuteronomic School* (Oxford: Clarendon Press, 1972) 235-36.

[44] For his reforming activity, see 2 Chron 17:7-9 where Jehoshaphat is reported to have sent officials to teach people in Judah from the book of the law of YHWH. M. Weinfeld, "Judge and Officer in the Ancient Near East and in Ancient Israel," *IOS* 7 (1977) 83, compares this to the Assyrian custom of sending officers to instruct communities in the "service of God and the king."

[45] *Supra.*, note 18, and Macholz, "Justizorganization," 318-21.

On the other hand, it is historically more probable that a king in
Judah (or Israel) would undertake such an administrative reorganization
than that these or similar changes were instituted much earlier in the
nation's history as stated in Exod 18:13-27 and Deut 1:9-17. It is also
more probable from a political and sociological perspective.
Wellhausen's argument from Jehoshaphat's name is not decisive against
a historical basis in the mid-ninth century either; one could argue that it
was a throne name given to the Judaean king because of the reforming
activity of his father Asa (2 Chron 15:1-16), and that Jehoshaphat
continued in his father's footsteps.

Extra-biblical parallels have been proposed as confirmation of the
Chronicler's authenticity concerning the reform account.[46]   The
problem of historical authenticity is *not* the feasibility of such a reform
in the mid-ninth century--that is certainly a historical possibility--it is
the relationship of this particular account to other biblical traditions and
social institutions that is of importance. Viewed in this light, the
account in 2 Chron is similar in some aspects to Exod 18:13-27 and
Deut 1:9-17 and, as we shall suggest, provides information
supplementary to these two accounts.

To begin with, the appointment of local judges is a consistent
tradition among the three accounts, although their locations are
described somewhat differently. Exod 18:21 and Deut 1:13 place these
judges generally with the people. Deut 16:18 places them "in all your

---

46   W. F. Albright, "The Judicial Reform of Jehoshaphat,"
Alexander Marx Jubilee Volume (ed. S. Lieberman; Philadelphia: Jewish
Publication Society, 1950) 78-80, draws a parallel with the Egyptian
judicial reform of Heremhab in the fourteenth century, where social
conditions under the eighteenth dynasty had disintegrated because of
corrupt officials. His goal in this study is to rehabilitate the Chronicler
as an historian on certain points and specifically to suggest the
reliability of the Chronicler's account of Jehoshaphat's reform.
Weinfeld's treatment in "Judge and Officer," is a thorough collection of
Near-Eastern parallels to the royal appointment of judges in ancient
Israel. He demonstrates in some detail that a common tradition of royal
officers and judges existed in the Near East (Hittites, Mari, Neo-
Assyrians) from the mid-second millennium. Largely on this basis he
concludes, "The quest for the historical setting of the traditions in Exod
18:13-27; Deut 1:9-18, 16:18-20, 17:8-13 and 2 Chron 19 is senseless"
(88)! Weinfeld thinks there were national judges in the premonarchical
period in Israel and that an appeals court early in the nation's history
presents no basic historical problems.

gates," perhaps an inclusive phrase for cities. The Chronicler places these judges in fortified cities implying a close relationship between the military organization and the state's administrative/judicial system, an important point to compare with Exod 18:21 and Deut 1:15. According to the Chronicler, Jehoshaphat also placed some military forces in these fortified cities of Judah. With regard to the military relationship, therefore, the Chronicler is in essential agreement with these two accounts, while Deut 16:18 actually seems to increase the number of local judges in its reference to their placement "in all your gates."[47]

Knierim argued in his treatment of Exod 18 that placing judges initially in the garrisons would unsettle a local judicial system the least because the newer system was structured along with the military organization already implemented in certain cities.[48] Macholz supplements this valid insight by pointing out that the king always had the uncontested authority in military affairs and Jehoshaphat's initial measures were merely a delegation of this authority to appointed officials.[49] Both of these observations suggest that the appointment of judges in the fortified cities, who may already have been military officers, is the earlier precedent from which the further appointment of judges "in all your gates" (Deut 16:18) is based.

---

[47]   Macholz ("Justizorganization," 335) thinks this aspect of the Dtr reform, where local judges are chosen, continues the use of royal judges instituted earlier but excludes the influence of the king.

[48]   Knierim, "Neuordnung," 163, 167 and note 169.

[49]   Macholz, "Justizorganization," 323-24; W. Rudolph, Chronikbücher(HAT 21; Tübingen, J. C. B. Mohr, 1955) 257-58, argues that placing these judges in the fortified cities predates the Dtr reform but that much of the other material given by the Chronicler presupposes the conditions of the post-exilic period. One function of the appointed judges, according to him, would be to deal with the problems between the garrisoned military forces and the local community. This is an important observation and quite probably true. The problem over property rights evidenced in the book of Micah may very well result from the conflicts between the military forces garrisoned in the Shephelah, who were commanded by the $r\bar{o}$'$\check{s}\bar{i}m$ and $q\bar{a}\check{s}\bar{i}n$, and the local populace. Furthermore, if the $r\bar{o}$'$\check{s}\bar{i}m$ also functioned as royal administrative/judicial officers as they are presented in Exod 18:25 and Deut 1:15, then one can easily understand why their oppressive schemes (Mic 3:1-4) were so effective.

A textual problem in v 8 obscures the role of the central court--an institution described in Deut 17:8-13 and implied in Exod 18:26 and Deut 1:17. The verse concludes in the MT, "to decide and they (the court) returned (to) Jerusalem." Not only does this clause make little sense, but the implication that the court was peripatetic seems unfounded. A slight change in the punctuation of the verb to *yōšebû*, reading "they presided in Jerusalem," is one possibility. The Septuagint reading suggests a slight change to *ûlrîbê yōšebê*, reading "and the cases of the inhabitants of Jerusalem." This rendering is problematic because the function of the court is clearly to hear difficult cases referred to it from other areas. It is best to repoint the MT and interpret the clause as a reference to the court's "presiding" (sitting) in Jerusalem even if it seems redundant to say so.[50] This reconstruction basically agrees with Deut 17:8, 10 that the central court was located in a place chosen by YHWH (i.e., Jerusalem).

The make-up of this court and the divisions of its responsibilities are described in terminology relevant to the post-exilic setting of the Chronicler. Verse 8 presupposes a distinction between priests and levites which seems indicative of the post-exilic period as probably does the reference to the chief priest in v 11. The division of responsibility between matters of the king and those of YHWH could mean nothing more than a simple division of labor, but the vocabulary is paralleled only in another passage from the Chronicler (1 Chron 26:20-32) and perhaps reflects the time of Zerubbabel and Joshua.[51] Zebadiah's title as *nāgîd* is also problematic. It is an old title (1 Sam 9:16)[52] and not the normal title for governor in the post-exilic period. On the other hand, it is a title used by the Chronicler at least twenty times in various contexts, so that its occurrence in v 11 is likely to be an example of an archaizing tendency by the writer. Finally, the reference to the levites as subordinate court-administrators or *šōṭerîm* is probably post-exilic in fact even though the title occurs elsewhere (Deut 16:18; Num 11:16) in similar contexts. In these other two references, the *šōṭerîm* are involved in the local administrative system not the central court, and there is no indication in them that these officials are levites.

---

50   With Macholz, "Justizorganization," 321 and note 12a.

51   Whitelam, *Just King*, 202.

52   Rudolph (*Chronikbücher*, 257) felt the use of this old title is the second reason why the Chronicler's account is not pure etiology.

There are two important preliminary conclusions to be drawn from this account of Jehoshaphat's reform. (1) An account of the placing of judges in fortified cities had no historical relevance in the period of the Chronicler, but it agrees with the other, older sources in relating military organization and judicial administration. This aspect has a good claim to historical reliability as an important facet of monarchical rule. (2) A central court of some format in Jerusalem also has a good claim to authenticity although its constitution is described with vocabulary and ideas more appropriate to the Chronicler and thus is largely anachronistic.[53]

The question of the silence of the DtrH concerning Jehoshaphat's reform in the treatment accorded the king's reign remains. There is a brief allusion to reforming activity and the usual notation that information may be found in the Chronicles of the Judaean kings (1 Kings 22:45-46), but no mention of a judicial reform. This silence should *not* be taken to mean the DtrH was unaware of a state appointed administrative/judicial system. On the contrary, Deut 1:9-18, 16:18 and 17:8-13 are part of the deuteronomistic corpus and they do record information on both the local appointment of judges and the workings of the dual court system. Evidently the writer(s) felt, as did the author of Exod 18:13-27, that it would be inappropriate theologically to attribute such a move to a king[54] rather than Moses the lawgiver.

All of these accounts of judicial reorganization examined in this chapter should be considered as evidence for the development of a state administrative/judicial system in the pre-exilic period. The account of Exod 18:13-27 is almost certainly older than the deuteronomistic material which neglects Jethro's role in advising Moses. While the Chronicler elaborates on both accounts with anachronisms, he does preserve two important pieces of information: that a Judaean king was responsible for a major reorganization in administrative/judicial practice and that initially the reorganization was based in the fortified cities with garrisoned troops where the king, as Knierim rightly suggested, had unquestioned authority. Some additional observations about this

---

[53]   A full discussion on the role of the priests in the central court and the nature of this body as an appeals court is not necessary. See the discussion in Whitelam (*Just King*, 197-203).

[54]   It is possible that Wellhausen and others are correct that the account is an etiology and the reform is attributed to Jehoshaphat on account of his name; if so, then the reform measures should be attributed to another early Judaean king.

"military connection" and the king's personal judicial authority need to be made before these factors can be correlated with what has already been deduced from the prophetical literature.

As discussed earlier in the chapter, "judging Israel" in the pre-monarchical period connoted the combination of military and administrative leadership as well as specifically judicial authority. The military associations of "judging" reflect early tribal history in the struggle against Philistine and east-Jordanian oppression. When a king is requested, it is acknowledged that he will judge and fight battles (1 Sam 8:20). During the early phases of the monarchy this association of military and judicial supremacy was embodied in the king himself. The various accounts about David's rise to power make it clear that he was a military genius. A major factor in his success was his employment of mercenaries whose loyalty was first to David and not to a particular tribe or state.[55] This fact of personal loyalty remained important because as the empire grew, so did the professional army. Solomon's many projects required professional soldiers with a chariot corps which set the standard for the kingdoms of the divided monarchy. He also established administrative districts (1 Kings 4:7-19) for tax collection purposes in order to finance his expenditures.[56] The governing system for these provinces is a clear indication of a newly emerging social structure for the tribes under statehood; each province had a governor (niṣṣāb) who was responsible to a central governor in Jerusalem who, in turn, was one of Solomon's cabinet officials (1 Kings 4:5a).

Virtually every surviving tradition about the united monarchy presents the king exercising the right to judge in certain cases that involve his personal affairs, military problems and state business. Probably he served as a court of appeal in certain cases.[57] For example, one important factor in Absalom's rebellion was the king's

---

[55]   B. Mazar, "The Military Elite of King David," *VT* 13 (1963) 310-20. The importance of a private army can be seen before the institution of kingship in early Israel; cf. M. Miller, "Saul's Rise to Power: Some Observations Concerning 1 Sam 9:1-10:16, 10:26-11:15," *CBQ* 36 (1974) 157-74, esp. 172-73.

[56]   On the administrative districts see G. E. Wright, "The Provinces of Solomon," *EI* 8 (1967) 58-68; Y. Aharoni, "The Provinces of Solomon," *TA* 3 (1976) 5-15.

[57]   For the king's judicial authority, *supra*, note 17.

son serving as a hearer of suits and as *de facto* "judge in the land" (2 Sam 15:1-6). Evidently David's case-load, like that depicted for Moses at Sinai, was more than he could adequately handle and Absalom had success in undermining his father's authority. It should be noted that there is no cabinet level official named as a judge in any list of officials for the united monarchy, implying that the traditional local assembly functioned apart from any direct action by the king or his designated representative. The institutional changes we have proposed for the mid-ninth century were a logical outgrowth of the expanding central authority and its duties.

The transition reconstructed for the administrative/judicial system is essentially a movement from a clan or village system of gate proceedings, later supplemented by the monarch who "judges" as the commander of the army and as YHWH's anointed, to a bi-level state structure[58] consisting of designated officials at both the regional and central levels. Local assemblies of elders continued to function as the book of Deuteronomy makes clear. Their duties, judicial authority, and power of sanction were probably curtailed in some instances by this state system that overlay the local assembly. One should point out that this bi-level state structure is very similar to the organization of the provincial system of Solomon, and that much the same can be said for the army's leaders, whose various ranks of people (cf. 1 Kings 9:22) served the king under the authority of a commander in the king's cabinet.

The military organization under the monarchy reflected the growing shift of power toward the capitals and fortified cities. It is quite understandable if not appropriate that further administrative/judicial developments would work through this structure. Many who functioned as officers in the levy, whether they were considered professional soldiers or not, were also elders and family heads so that, ideally speaking, the complicated fact for a local community of dealing with central authority would be lessened somewhat by having some of their own as appointed officials.

It is important to note that Jehoshaphat's reform only dealt with Judah. In comparing the material from Isaiah and Micah with that from

---

58   Macholz ("Justizorganization," 331) described Jehoshaphat's system as a *Verstaatlichung der Rechtspflege*. To call this system "bi-level" is to acknowledge it functioned on both a central and regional level.

these accounts of reorganization two things stand out in general agreement. (1) Officials with titles are responsible for the administrative/judicial system. In Isaiah it is the *śārîm* and the *zeqānîm* who judge corruptly. The guilty officials of Isa 10:1 are not named but their perceived crimes are similar in nature to those ascribed to the *śārîm* in Isa 1:23. In Micah those responsible for *in*justice are titled *rō'šîm* and *qāṣîn*, and are national officers (3:1, 9, 11a). (2) Every relevant title in the prophetical texts also occurs in the accounts of administrative/judicial reorganization except the *qāṣîn* of Micah. This congruence is significant. Both Isaiah and Micah provide positive evidence that some form of state control in administrative/judicial affairs existed in the eighth century--a crucial point to remember in assessing a historical basis for Jehoshaphat's reform. Indeed, what could be concluded from the investigation of the prophetical literature about the existence and influence of a state administrative/judicial system in Chapter One is largely confirmed by these other accounts. Perhaps the major ecxeption to this conclusion is the perception of corruption which comes from the prophets alone.

One can easily understand how the state administrative/judicial system, almost certainly instituted for reasons of uniformity and efficiency, would lead to tension and divided loyalties among its constituents. On the officials' side, their position and perhaps livelihood depended on the favor of their superiors, while local citizens could find that more and more decisions about their own livelihood (and specifically their property rights!) were rendered by those whose authority was not subject to local custom or influence.[59] If this reconstruction is correct, then it is also understandable why the administrative/judicial corruption was often perceived as "legal," rather efficient in its unfortunate habits, and why concerned individuals seemed powerless to effect change. There seems to have been little check or balance on the authority of the central government, and this seems to apply as well to its designated representatives and officials. The prophetic accusations in the name of YHWH over the abuse of property rights may come partly from this realization and hence represent a divine judgment where human sanctions were inadequate.

---

[59]   Chapter Four will deal with the rights and privileges of the state officials.

Additional evidence for the development of the judicial system in the northern kingdom is fragmentary.[60] In all probability the state had similar institutions like Judah. There is evidence, for example, that Israel too had been divided into districts (1 Kings 20:14-15) as the reference to the officers of the districts, *śārê hammedīnôt*, makes clear. In 2 Kings 4:13 Elisha offers a Shunamite woman his intercession on her behalf with an unnamed army commander *(śar ṣābā')* suggesting that military personnel did have civilian administrative affairs as their responsibility along with other duties.[61] As noted earlier, Hos 13:10 confirms that Israel had *śārīm* and *šōpeṭīm* who were closely related to royal policy, and Amos provides explicit evidence for the pervasive influence of Samaria's administrative policies upon the nation. Thus the circumstances of tension posited for Judah would be similar in nature to those in Israel.

Summary and Conclusions

The chapter began by considering some references in the eighth-century prophets to the judicial court system and its administrators. The texts provided a secure chronological frame, some specific titles of officials and the perception that the court system was a primary contribution to the loss of property rights. To this must be added a conclusion previously reached in Chapter One on the prophetical literature that titled officials and others in positions of influence were generally responsible for the perceive loss of property rights; the court system was a prominent example of a more fundamental perception.

---

60   Whitelam (*Just King*, 167-84) discusses most of the evidence. The lengthy narrative about Naboth's fate in 1 Kings 21 is not designed to inform the audience about normal judicial procedure but to show Ahab's (and Jezebel's) guilt in his execution. Yet the narrative does take for granted the function of the local assembly, the position of elders and nobles *(ḥōrīm)* in assembling the people, and the close ties between these officials and the monarchy.

61   Jehu's letters (2 Kings 10:1-7) to the elders and *śārīm* of Samaria presupposes that these people control the chariots and fortified cities in the area. The historical context is one of a *coup d'etat* in progress so that the duties of these officials in this instance are not decisive evidence for the normal state of administrative/judicial affairs and responsibilities.

In tracing some developments in the state administrative/judicial system, in was concluded that under the divided monarchy judges and certain other officials served in an appointed capacity exercising judicial authority and performing general administrative duties. What was attributed to Moses in Exod 18:13-27--i.e., the appointment of these officials--was actually a warrant for some later monarch(s). The eighth-century prophets presuppose some such system as does the book of Deuteronomy, with the latter perhaps contributing some measures of reform or change. For Judah, the account of Jehoshaphat's administrative/judicial organization provides a few important details in spite of several anachronisms and fits the proposed chronological scheme. What evidence exists suggests that Israel too had a similar system by the eighth century. The best reconstruction for both kingdoms is that under the monarchy a type of bi-level administrative/judicial system based on state appointment and authority developed that gradually curtailed the authority of the local assembly in certain instances.

Various official titles from the prophetic texts occur also in the accounts of administrative/judicial reform. While the titles (officials) are of a general nature, nevertheless this significant fact is evidence that the same type of personnel is involved in both contexts. The culprits of the prophets' accusations are not simply the anonymous rich and powerful in a community but are those who benefit from official status and position. The accounts of reform add the fact of a military connection for many of these officials in addition to their administrative/judicial duties. Exod 18:21, 25, Deut 1:15 and probably 2 Chron 19:5, imply these appointees were leaders of the loosely organized people's army or general military levy. This too is significant because, as required for an efficient army, these officials owed their loyalty first to the king and received much of their authority from him. Any necessary power for enforcement was readily available and backed by military force. In assessing the implications of this reconstruction, one important point stands out immediately: there is little evidence of a check or balance on the authority of the central government in general and specifically with regard to its designated representatives and officials. The prophetic accusations in the name of YHWH over the abuse of property rights may partly come from this realization and, as concluded earlier, represent a divine judgment where human sanctions were inadequate.

There is another important point to be made from this research that relates directly to the first chapter: nothing in the data examined concerning the administrative/judicial system implies that either its administrators, structure, or policies are specifically "Canaanite" and therefore a perversion of Israelite custom.[62]   If anything, the development we reconstructed shows the growth of a system that depended on royal appointment and policy, often with *Israelite* clan and military leaders as administrators, that nevertheless had some unfortunate consequences according to the prophets.

This line of investigation has been concerned with the administrative/judicial system and its effects on property rights. Important facets of the system have been elucidated and some background for perspective provided, yet little information has been gained about property rights themselves. There are, however, several things to note in summary form. It appears from this investigation that the usual place for adjudication was the gate of a city as stated in Amos 5:10-12, Deut 16:18, *etc.* Evidently the gate of a city was the focal point for administrative concerns regardless of who wielded the authority. Land sales would be witnessed and confirmed there among other community affairs and personal concerns needing adjudication. The accusation that justice was not being done in the gate (so Amos)[63] or more generally that the administrative/judicial system was corrupt would be directed at those who functioned as judges and administrators. We have concluded that such officials received their authority and appointment from the king. Whether these appointees were, at times, local elders or whether, once appointed, they could effectively make decisions regardless of local approval is not definitely known. Probably

---

[62]   Some scholars believe the administrative system developed under David and Solomon had Canaanite officials and practices for its basis; so Donner, "Die soziale Botschaft," 229-45, who is dependent upon Alt. Cf. Donner's unpublished dissertation, *Studien zur Verfassungs und Verwaltungsgeschichte der Reiche Israel und Juda* (Leipzig, 1956).

[63]   Koch ("Die Entstehung," 246) correctly stated that those Amos accused of injustice were not under the authority of the local assembly in the gate. His assertion, however, that the entrance of citizens into debt slavery required no word from the assembly seems wrong. The gate itself is a place of corruption, implying those ruling there are held responsible for injustice. Secondly, entrance into debt slavery sometimes required the sale of land which seems to have required, in turn, public witness and confirmation in the gate (Gen 23:18; Ruth 4:1-11).

both suppositions are correct. Moses' appointments are taken from among the people (Exod 18:25; Deut 1:13), and the prophetic perception of widespread, effective corruption is not likely apart from the ability to override local disapproval.

Excursus One

The Yabneh Yam Letter

A letter discovered on the coast of Israel provides epigraphic evidence for judicial appeal in pre-exilic Israel, the type of official involved in adjudication, and an example of a garment seized in a dispute (cf. Amos 2:8a; Mic 2:8b). The seventh century document was found at Yabneh Yam (Mesad Hashavyahu) in a storeroom beside the gate of a fortress.[64]   The following English translation is that of W. F. Albright.[65]   Specific references to this appeal or "lawsuit"[66] in the excursus contain the Hebrew text in transliteration.

Let my lord commander hear the case of his servant. As for thy servant, thy servant was harvesting at Hazarsusim. And thy servant was still harvesting as they finished the storage of grain, as usual before the Sabbath.   While thy servant was finishing the storage of grain with his harvesters, Hoshaiah son of Shobai came and took thy servant's mantle. It was while I was finishing with my harvesters that this one for no reason took thy servant's mantle. And all my companions will testify on my behalf--those who were harvesting with me in the heat...all my companions will testify on my behalf. If I am innocent of guilt, let him return my mantle, and if not, it is still the commander's right to take my case under advisement and to send word to him asking that he return the mantle of thy servant.   And let not the plea of his servant be displeasing to him.

---

64   J. Naveh, "A Hebrew Letter from the Seventh Century B. C.," *IEJ* 10 (1960) 129-39, has the archaeological details as well as an interpretation.   For the text, see *KAI* 1, 36, and for a detailed philological study, D. Pardee, "The Judicial Plea from Mesad Hashavjahu (Yavneh Yam): A New Philological Study," *Maarav* 1 (1978-79) 33-66.

65   *ANET*, 568.

66   V. Sasson, "An Unrecognized Juridical Term in the Yabneh Yam Lawsuit and in an Unnoticed Biblical Parallel," *BASOR* 232 (1978) 57-74.

The document is fragmentary (Albright's translation is, in part, conjecture) but is apparently an appeal by a worker to an official *('dny hśr)* requesting that a garment taken from him by a certain Hoshaiah be returned. The plea states, *wyb' hś'yhw bn šb wyqḥ 't bgd 'bdk* "and Hoshaiah son of Shobai came and took your servant's garment." The sender of the letter was a reaper *(qṣr)*, probably serving as a conscripted laborer. Perhaps the dispute involved a quota owed by the writer and/or expected by Hoshaiah.

This letter draws on terminology from Israel's legal traditions so that it has been termed more precisely a "lawsuit." A formal appeal supported by a protestation of innocence is made to the official *(śār)* at the fortress. In this letter, as in the prophetic literature of the eighth century, no appeal is made to an existing statute although pentateuchal legislation exists which would prohibit such a seizure (Exod 22:25-27; Deut 24:10-13). Appeal is made on the basis of innocence in the dispute. The writer asks for the return of the garment, stating that it was seized over a misunderstanding and points out that his rights of possession had been violated.

This epigraphic evidence is important for several reasons. (1) It provides a clear context for the seizure of a garment, an act twice mentioned in prophetic accusations. (2) This seventh-century document contains no appeal to any laws in the Pentateuch prohibiting the seizure of such a garment. A similar phenomenon can be observed as late as Nehemiah 5, where the lending of money or provisions at interest is not condemned as illegal by a reference to pentateuchal legislation. (3) The role of the fortress commander *(śār)* in adjudicating the dispute appears to confirm the conclusion drawn in Chapter Three about the role of the *śārīm*. Evidently the fortress *śār* had the dual role of military commander and administrator/judge for judicial appeal. Indirectly, the letter suggests that the fortress and its commander played an important role in the local economy through labor projects (corvée), harvest schedules and the levy.

Chart Three

The Administrative/Judicial System

Text	People Appointed	Duties
Exod 18:13-27	heads *(roʾšīm)* officials *(śārīm)*	local judges, refer all hard cases to Moses
Num 11:16 17, 24-30	elders *(zeqānīm)* officials *(šōṭerīm)*	prophecy, assist with the administrative burden
Deut 1: 9-18	heads *(rōʾšīm)*, officials *(śārīm, šōṭerīm)* judges *(šōpeṭīm)*	local judges, refer hard matters to Moses
Deut 16:18	judges *(šōpeṭīm)* officers *(šōṭerīm)*	local judges
Deut 17: 8-13	levitical priests, a judge *(šōpēṭ)*	rule on difficult cases brought to them
2 Chron 19:4-11	judges *(šōpeṭīm)*, in Jerusalem-- levites, priests, heads *(rōʾšīm)*, chief "judge" *(nāgīd)*, chief- priest *(kōhēn harōʾš)*	central court rules on difficult matters con- cerning YHWH and the king

Chapter Four

Royal Officials and Property Rights

In previous chapters, something of the role of royal officials in ancient Israel has been reconstructed. The prophets repeatedly accuse them (and others) of injustice and of using their status and position to circumvent the property rights of others. Some aspects of their functions and duties were investigated in Chapter Three, demonstrating in particular that their authority in administrative/judicial matters was derived from the king.

This chapter will discuss the privileges of the king and his officials in more detail, especially with regard to their property rights, along with some other references to their duties. In addition to the influence of the administrative/judicial system, the property rights *extended* to royal officials such as land grants and income from taxation also conflicted with the perceived rights of other citizens. This perception-- and a list of royal privileges--is found in 1 Sam 8:11-17 and will be a focal point of investigation. 1 Sam 8:11-17 is also important because it provides additional evidence for the close relationship between a king and his appointed officials as discussed in Chapter Three.

1 Samuel 8:11-17

11 And he said, 'this will be the right of the king when he rules over you: He will take your sons and place them with his chariot and with his horsemen and they will run before his chariot;

12 And he will appoint for himself commanders of thousands and commanders of fifties and (some) to do his plowing and to reap his harvest and to make weapons of war and for his chariot.

13 And he will take your daughters for perfumers, cooks and bakers;

14 And the best of your fields and vineyards and olive groves he will take and give (them) to his servants.

15 And he will take a tenth of your grain and vineyards and give (them) to his officers and servants;

16   The best of your male and female servants, and your cattle[1]
and donkeys he will take and use for his work;

17   He will take a tenth of your sheep and you will be his
servants.'

This list of royal privileges is embedded in a chapter dealing with
the failure of Samuel's sons as judges and the people's request in v 5 for
a king "like all the nations."   The corruption of Samuel's sons is
depicted as the taking of bribes and perverting justice (yaṭṭû mišpāṭ).
The use of the verb nṭh in this context is similar to its use in
accusations in Amos (2:7, 5:12) and Isaiah (10:2, 29:21).   Samuel is
represented as taking the people's request personally but is assured by
YHWH that it is he not Samuel who is ultimately is being rejected.   At
YHWH's command, Samuel testifies to the consequences of their choice
and accedes to their wishes for a monarch when the people refuse to
reconsider.

Since the detailed source analysis of Wellhausen,[2] chapter 8 has
been assigned to a later, antimonarchical source reflecting exilic
disillusionment with human kinship. Along with chapter 12, chapter 8
functions as a bracket to various older traditions in an earlier source
(9:1-10:16, 11:1-15) that was more favorable to kingship.[3]   The later
source's historical reliability, including chapter 8, was assessed by
Wellhausen as one where "there cannot be a word of truth in the whole
narrative."[4]   Noth's influential work on the Deuteronomistic history
agreed that chapter 8 was part of a later source and concluded that it was
"durch und durch deuteronomistisch formuliert."[5]

---

[1]   With the Septuagint. MT has "young men."

[2]   J. Wellhausen, *Die Composition des Hexateuchs und der
historischen Bücher des Alten Testaments* (Berlin: Georg Reimer, 1889)
243-44.

[3]   See O. Eissfeldt, *The Old Testament. An Introduction* (Oxford:
Basil Blackwell, 1965) 268-81, for the various opinions on sources and
monarchical views.

[4]   Wellhausen, *Prolegomena*, 249.

[5]   M. Noth, *Uberlieferungsgeschichtliche Studien* (Tübingen: Max
Niemeyer, 1957) 57. Alt ("Der Anteil," 356) also attributed 1 Sam 8 to a
late source.

The views of Wellhausen and Noth have generally prevailed among scholars. Recently, however, several scholars have taken exception to Wellhausen's historical assessment and Noth's conclusions about a thorough Deuteronomistic formulation of chapter 8.[6]   Crüsemann and Birch, for example, have correctly pointed out that *nothing* in vs 11-17 is typically Deuteronomistic.   A better case for Deuteronomistic formulation can be made for vs 4-10, 18-22.   Even Clements, who is prepared to agree with much of Noth's evaluation, nevertheless insists that vs 11-17 were only incorporated and not compiled by the Deuteronomistic historians "since we should certainly have expected them to stress the potentially disastrous religious and political consequences of his(the king) disobedience to Yahweh and disobedience to the divine law."[7]

In agreeing with Clements and others, one cannot simply accept at face-value that the king in Israel would or did act in such a manner as described in vs 11-17.   Such actions are indeed described as the king's right *(mišpāṭ)*.   Also, a similar statement in 1 Sam 10:25, where the *mišpāṭ hammelūkāh* for Saul is written in a book, implies that actual rights and privileges are in the author's mind. The description in vs 11-17, however, is polemical in tone and is best identified from a literary viewpoint as a parody.[8]   It is more likely that actual rights are distorted and exaggerated than that they are fabricated for theological reasons.

Once the view of exaggeration is accepted, then the historical circumstances of the pre-exilic period come into play.   Scholars have

---

[6]   R. Clements, "The Deuteronomistic Interpretation of the Founding of the Monarchy in 1 Sam VIII," *VT* 24 (1974) 398, lists several scholars as well as himself who hold this view.   In addition, Crüsemann, *Der Widerstand*, 60-66; and B. Birch, *The Rise of the Israelite Monarchy: The Growth and Development of I Samuel 7-15* (SBLDS 27; Missoula: Scholars Press, 1976) 21-28, have questioned the fact of a thorough Deuteronomistic redaction.

[7]   Clements, "I Sam VIII," 400.   Both Crüsemann (*Der Widerstand*, 66) and Birch (*Growth*, 113-14 and note 39) offer a reconstruction of the Hebrew original of vs 11-17 before its incorporation into a later source.

[8]   Crüsemann (*Der Widerstand*, 66 and footnote 1) has noted that vs 11-17 could be based on a similar, more neutral agreement between people and king.   But the passage as we have it, "es handelt sich um eine ausgesprochene Polemik; genau wie in der Jothamfabel liegt eine politische Kampfschrift vor " (70).

pointed to two cultural backgrounds against which this text can be viewed. (1) The practices of Canaanite kingship known from the tablets of Ugarit and Alalakh provide plentiful evidence of conscription, taxation, land grants, appropriations, *etc.*, so that Samuel's warning is not anachronistic but exaggerates actual circumstances in Syria/Palestine from the second millennium.[9] (2) The taxation and conscription policies of Solomon were a major factor in the division of the kingdom under Rehoboam, so that the text is exaggerating some actual practices of the Israelite monarchy.[10]

The first option has the advantage of providing a context in the late second millennium and thus assumes that the passage represents the views of Samuel himself and not some later writer. Those who advocate this view emphasize that policies in vs 11-17 are those of Canaanite or non-Israelite kingship, and that the request for a king like all the nations in v 5 is really a desire to become like citizens of socially stratified Canaanite city-states (cf. Exod 16:3). There are at least two convincing reasons to reject this interpretation. One is that the request for a king like all the nations is not necessarily bad or specifically Canaanite. The same request for a king like other nations receives a qualified approval in Deut 17:14-20. In this latter passage there are certain religious and social qualifications for kingship, including that the monarch not be a foreigner *(nōkrī),* but kingship itself is honored by YHWH. A second reason is that the passage is clearly depicting an Israelite king. The second person plural suffixes directly address Israelite property owners, a fact which could also provide an indication of the social classes from which such a tract originated.[11] Verse 18 indicates that a later author (the DtrH?) associated the enumeration of the king's rights with Israelite kingship: "In that day you will cry our from before your king whom you chose for yourselves, but YHWH will not answer you in that day."

The second option is supported rather than hindered by these reasons. As noted above, Solomon's administrative and fiscal policies

---

[9]   I. Mendelsohn, "Samuel's Denunciation of Kingship in the Light of the Akkadian Documents from Ugarit," *BASOR* 143 (1956) 17-22; S. Paul and W. Dever, *Biblical Archaeology* (New York: Quadrangle, 1974) 184-85; J. Mauchline, *1 and 2 Samuel* (NBC; London: Oliphants, 1971) 91-92; T. Mettinger, *Solomonic State Officials*, 82.

[10]   Clements, "I Sam VIII," 403-4; Crüsemann, *Der Widerstand*, 72-7.

[11]   Crüsemann, *Der Widerstand*, 72-73.

were certainly viewed by some in Israel as oppressive; in fact so oppressive that the kingdom collapsed over the continuation of his policies (1 Kings 12:1-20). The logical conclusion is that the practices parodied in vs 11-17 are those of Israelite and Judeaen kings of whom Solomon is the best known and one of the most deserving examples (cf. Jer 22:13-17).

Even as a parody, vs 11-17 are important as a list of (property) rights of the king and his servants. The subject matter of these rights can be subsumed under two general headings: military conscription and appropriations for royal service.[12] In v 11 the reference is to military conscription of the king's subjects, a well known practice in ancient and modern times. Both Absalom (2 Sam 15:1) and Adonijah (1 Kings 1:5) are pictured as employing chariots with fifty men as runners or escorts, which was probably typical for officers in the chariot corps. Verse 12 is a statement that the king will appoint commanders (*śārīm*) for his army. We noted in the previous chapter that kings in Israel appointed the *śārīm* as military leaders and judicial administrators. This passage is an indication of the way in which the ruler acquired loyalty; by exercising his prerogative to appoint commanders and to reward them with property he had appropriated.

The passage names several things the king would appropriate. In addition to conscription for military service, the list includes women and daughters for court service, agricultural workers for the royal estates, servants of property owners, and the latter's cattle, land and produce. Those appropriated or conscripted for non-military service were probably part of the corvée system. According to 2 Sam 20:24, there was forced labor in Israel as early as the reign of David. The information recorded for Solomon's corvée seems contradictory when one compares 1 Kings 5:27-32 with 1 Kings 9:15-22. The difficulty of the terminology is partially responsible;[13] however, an inconsistency still remains. The latter passage states of the corvée system that it was formed of non-Israelites because the Israelites themselves comprised the military forces. One wonders why Adoram, the minister of labor (*ʿal hammas),* was stoned to death by "all Israel" if Israelites were not

---

12   See generally, R. de Vaux, *Ancient Israel* (New York: McGraw Hill, 1965) 1. 141-42, 213-28.

13   As Mettinger (*Solomonic State Officials*, 128-39) maintains. His distinction between simple and permanent "forced levy," the difference between *mas* and *mas ʿōbēd,* is not entirely convincing.

conscripted for labor (1 Kings 12). While one cannot agree that an Israelite monarch arbitrarily took what he wanted for corvée labor, it must be concluded that some unpopular institutional measures were in effect in pre-exilic Israel for the royal benefit, including the conscription of Israelite citizens for various duties. Mic 3:10 and Jer 22:13 are probably prophetic reactions to such measures in Judah (cf. Chapter Three, Excursus One).

The description of land appropriation in v 14 is certainly an exaggeration. Even Ahab, who is vilified by the DtrH, could not simply take Naboth's land. His success in finally gaining the vineyard could, however, exemplify the kind of situation opposed by the author of vs 11-17. It has been conjectured with some persuasiveness that the property of criminals reverted to the crown upon conviction of certain crimes.[14] This would be the reason for trying Naboth on a trumped-up charge and having him executed. Zelophahad's daughters protested to Moses that they should get their father's land because he was not involved in Korah's rebellion (Num 27:3). The comment appears superfluous, yet it is completely relevant as an argument against an impediment to inheritance because of criminal charges. That a king acquired abandoned property is implied by the case of the Shunamite women in 2 Kings 8:1-6. A king had several ways of "acquiring" property that may have disgruntled some citizens. Perhaps the most pernicious would be through foreclosure, whereby a debtor would transfer title to his property in return for the amortizing of a debt. Nehemiah 5:4 is a later example that records the anguish of those who pledged fields and family members to pay the king's tax.

There is little doubt that the king had large land holdings.[15] Whether through conquest, inheritance, dowry, sale or grant, the royal property was extensive and required a staff for its management (1 Chron 27:25-31). It is this property that the conscripted agricultural workers of v 12 would tend. The royal estate is probably also the source of land that is granted to the king's servants.[16] Verse 14 represents the king as simply taking land and giving it to his servants. As noted above,

---

[14]   Ibid., 82 and footnote 15, citing possible parallels in Alalakh, no. 17, and Ugarit, PRU 16.145: cf. Whitelam (The Just King, 175-76).

[15]   M. Noth, "Das Krongut der israelitischen Könige und seine Verwaltung," ZDPV 50 (1927) 211-44.

[16]   In agreement with H. J. Stoebe, Das Erste Buch Samuelis (KAT 8/1; Gütersloh: Gerd Mohn, 1973) 188.

the arbitrary confiscation of land by the king himself is neither attested nor likely, much less for his servants who were dependent upon his authority for their positions. What is attested in the Hebrew Bible and in the ancient Near East[17] are land grants by a monarch to his appointed officials for their support. A good example is the case of Mephibosheth in 2 Sam 9. Evidently David appropriated Saul's property, but for the sake of Jonathan granted part of the property back to Saul's son Mephibosheth. When Absalom's rebellion broke out, Mephibosheth stayed in Jerusalem while David fled. The king retaliated by awarding the property to Mephibosheth's servant Ziba (2 Sam 16:4, 19:29). These grants make it clear that while the property was awarded by royal favor, the land was still ultimately part of the royal estate. Another text for consideration is 2 Sam 14:30, where Absalom tells an associate that he and Joab have fields, is likely a reference to part of the royal estate granted to them for support.

The clearest example or reference to the practice of land grants is found in the questions of Saul to the Benjaminites in 1 Sam 22:7: "Will the son of Jesse give each of you fields and vineyards, will he appoint you commanders of thousands and commanders of hundreds?" These questions are not rhetorical but assume that Saul, unlike David who commanded a band of debtors (1 Sam 22:2), could make such grants to his officers. Mendelsohn's study of 1 Sam 8 rejected the implication of this text and argued instead that Saul's questions "could not possibly have been based on his own practice of appointing his followers to high military rank and granting them crown lands... Saul drew his picture of the way of kingship from contemporary feudal Canaanite society."[18] Mendelsohn's opinion is based on the common but erroneous view that 1 Sam 8:11-17 refers to Canaanite practice which were opposed by Israelite custom. Such practices are by no means limited to Syro-Palestinian monarchs,[19] though vs 11-17 do have parallels in the "Canaanite" documents from Ugarit and Alalakh, nor does any reference in the Hebrew Bible forbid the practice to Israelite kings. Land grants are assumed as an Israelite and royal

---

[17]   A. F. Rainey, "The System of Land Grants at Ugarit in Its Wider Near Eastern Setting," *Fourth World Congress of Studies* (Jerusalem: World Congress of Jewish Studies, 1967) 1. 187-91.

[18]   Mendelsohn, "Samuel's denunciation," 22 and footnote 38.

[19]   J. N. Postgate, *Neo-Assyrian Royal Grants and Decrees* (Rome: Biblical Institute Press, 1969); *infra*, Excursus Two.

prerogative in 1 Sam 22:7, 2 Sam 9 and Ezek 46:16-18. This last passage is a late text which has certain similarities to 1 Sam 8:14. It is acknowledged in the passage that the prince *(nāśīʾ)* of the restored nation will make grants to his sons and servants. Reform measures are commanded, however, prohibiting the prince from taking "from the *naḥalāh* of the people to disposses them of their property. He shall make apportionment for his sons from his own property." This post-exilic (?) text is a bitter commentary on what was perceived or reported to have been pre-exilic practice, and while accepting the practice wishes to reform its nature and effects for the projected new community. Elsewhere in this visionary section of Ezekiel (45:9), the princes are commanded to "stop your evictions *(gerūšōtēkem)*."[20] Thus there is sufficient evidence for both the acceptance of the practice of land grants in Israel as well as evidence for the social problems associated with them.

The earlier prophets from the eighth century were not as explicit about the authority for forming landed estates as the visionary author of Ezek 45:8-9, 46:16-18; yet for whatever reasons they did oppose them. Some of the *latifundia* of the eighth century were probably formed through royal grants and approval. Obviously land accumulation resulted from several different circumstances, but a grant of land and taxation privileges (of collection and/or exemption) provided two important advantages in building an estate. The prominent role of officials in the prophets' accusations lends further support to the conclusion that these property rights of officials contributed significantly to the "woes" of Isa 5:8, Mic 2:1-4 and similar accusations.

Taxation in the form of a tithe is mentioned for the support of royal officials (v 15) and for the king (v 17). Lack of any clear parallels to this type of civil taxation has suggested to some that these references cannot be historically accurate for pre-exilic Israel.[21] While one can question the accuracy of these particular references,[22] it seems futile to

---

20   Cf. Mic 2:9 where the verb *grš* is used to describe the eviction of women and children from there homes.

21   O. Eissfeldt, *Erstlinge und Zehnten im Alten Testament* (BWANT I/22; Stuttgart: Kolhammer, 1917) 154.

22   Evidence that a tithe was collected at Ugarit does not prove the same for Israel. The Sargon Display Inscription records that when Samaria was taken the Assyrian king "imposed the tax of the(ir) former King upon them;" cited in M. Cogan *Imperialism and Religion: Assyria,*

question the fact of taxation in the pre-exilic period. Solomon's provincial system (1 Kings 4:7-19) and probably David's census (2 Sam 24:1-9) were concerned with the collection of revenue for the state. Otherwise, the historical books record such exactions as tolls (1 Kings 10:14-15), assessment (2 Kings 23:33, 35),[23] tribute (2 Chron 17:11)[24] and presents (2 Chron 17:5).[25] The important thing for the present topic is the close relationship between the support for royal officials and taxation. There can be little doubt that this is a crucial relationship for understanding the conflict over property rights in the eighth century. In some instances, even terminology employed by the prophets is identical to or cognate with the language of the historical books. Amos 2:8 and 5:11 are two examples containing references to exactions of wine and wheat respectively.[26] Both appear to be taxes of some kind and their effects are bitterly opposed by the prophet. Isaiah's description of Judah's leaders as taskmasters (nōgeśīm) in 3:12 employs a term also used for tribute collection in 2 Kings 23:35 or for a debt collector in Deut 15:2-3. A reference in the same verse to these leaders as usurers confirms that state and private exactions are in the prophet's mind. This pattern is found elsewhere in the ancient Near East where officials gained support through taxation and used their material means to become creditors as well.[27]

One can describe the land-grant and taxation system as a practice designed to distribute property for patronage and state security. While the system and part of its effects can be traced through references in the Hebrew Bible, there is fragmentary epigraphical evidence from Israel and Judah that apparently shows the system in operation. Both the Samaria

---

Judah and Israel in the Eighth and Seventh Centuries B. C. E. (SBLMS 19; Missoula: Scholars Press, 1974) 101 and footnote 22.

23   Two different words are used: in v 33 the noun ʿōnaš is used (cf. Amos 2:8, 2 Kings 10:15 in Septuagint) and v 35 has the verb ʿrk in the hiphil.

24   The Hebrew is maśśāʾ (cf. Amos 5:11).

25   The Hebrew is minḥāh.

26   *Supra.*, notes 23-24.

27   E.g., at Alalakh a high government official was able to control much of the city through loans with high interest rates and severe security clauses; cf. D. J. Wiseman, *The Alalakh Tablets* (London: British Institute of Archaelogy at Ankara, 1953) 2-3. There are examples from Neo-Assyria as well, *infra*, Excursus Two.

Ostraca and the Judaean *lmlk* stamps are frequently associated with the royal estate, land-grants and taxation. It is to this important evidence that we now turn before summarizing our conclusions.

Samaria Ostraca

These ostraca are inscribed potsherds which record shipments of commodities to Samaria.[28]   Since their discovery by the Harvard excavation team at *Sebaste*, their interpretation has evoked a considerable discussion about their date and purpose.[29]

At least sixty-five ostraca were found on the floor of a storeroom but the stratigraphy at the time of discovery was imprecisely known. It seems, however, that stratum IV is a likely candidate,[30] which agrees with the consensus of ceramic typology and palaeography to place the documents in an eighth-century context. The ostraca were floor debris or possibly fill, implying that they had served their purpose and had been discarded.[31]   They were probably the ancient equivalent of the "scratch pad" upon which a quick notation could be made until a more official record (papyrus?) could be completed.[32]

There are twenty-four ostraca dated to the year 15, one to the year 17, and twenty-four dated to the years 9 or 10. Several ostraca contain no dates. Two basic formulas are employed in the ostraca with some minor variations (cf. category 2 below).

I (no 18)	II (no. 22)
A. in year 10	A. in year 15
B. from Hazeroth	B. from Helek
C. to *(l)* Gadiyau	C. to *(l)* Asa (ben) Ahimelek
D. a jar of fine oil	D. Helez

---

[28]   G. A. Reisner *et al.*, *Harvard Excavations at Samaria 1908-10* (Cambridge: Harvard University Press, 1924) 1. 227-46.

[29]   A. Lemaire, *Inscriptions Hebraiques*, 25-81.

[30]   Kenyon, *Samaria-Sebaste* III, 470.

[31]   Lemaire, *Inscriptions*, 39-40. From the different dates inscribed on the sherds, it is clear that the ostraca were received at different times.

[32]   A. Rainey, "The *Sitz im Leben* of the Samaria Ostraca," *TA* 6 (1979) 91.

E. from Hazeroth

At least three things seem clear from studying these formulas. (1) The year 15 is written in a hieratic numeral used elsewhere in Iron Age Palestine.[33]   (2) The name Helek in IIB is found in the Hebrew Bible as are several other names found in the sending position. They are known from the clan names of Manasseh listed in Num 26:30-33, Josh 17: 2-3 and 1 Chron 7:14-19. (3) The ostraca dated from the year 15 or 17 have different names for recipients (position C) in comparison with those dated from years 9 or 10. Because of the complete name changes, and the fact that the two forms divide rather easily between years 9-10 on the one hand and year 15 on the other, some scholars have concluded the changes represent a span of more than six years. Of course, this is based on the assumption that the names of the recipients would not totally change in just six years. Thus years 9-10 would refer to the reign of Joash and those from years 15 or 17 to that of Jeroboam II, the only king in Israel of the eighth century to rule fifteen years or more.[34] This reconstruction agrees with the archaeological context of the ostraca's discovery and is the best solution to the problem of dating.

The general purpose of the ostraca is clear: to record the shipments of commodities to a royal storehouse in Samaria. Those whose names are prefaced with a Lamed *(l)*[35] are thus associated with Samaria as

---

[33]   Y. Aharoni, "The Use of Hieratic Numerals in Hebrew Ostraca and the Shekel Weights." *BASOR* 184 (1966) 13-19.

[34]   The census of Jeroboam is a likely reason for the switch to clan names (1 Chron 5:17) and could be the occasion for the taxation policies opposed by Amos. W. Shea, "The Date and Purpose of the Samaria Ostraca," *IEJ* 27 (1977) 21-22, has argued that Pekah also ruled for 20 years (2 Kings 15:27) and that the ostraca dated to the 15th or 17th years should be assigned to his reign. The text of 2 Kings 15:27 contains a secondary tradition and an incorrect date. Pekah could not possibly have ruled that long; cf. K. T. Andersen, "Die Chronologie der Könige von Israel und Juda," *ST* 23 (1969) 98.

[35]   Y. Yadin, "Recipients or Owners. A Note on the Samaria Ostraca," *IEJ* 9 (1959) 184-87, suggests that the lamed *(l)* which prefixed personal names on the ostraca represents owners who are sending their produce to Samaria, not recipients already in the city. It has been shown, however, that *l* signifies a recipient in both Ugaritic and Hebrew literature, especially where the exchange of property is concerned; cf. A. Rainey, "Administration in Ugarit and the Samaria Ostraca," *IEJ* 12

well. Three basic interpretations of the specific purpose of the ostraca have been proposed.[36]

(1)   Taxes or Tithes. Support for an interpretation which considers them as tithes paid to a religious institution could be derived from Amos 4:4, but the lack of any discovered temple at Samaria plus the many named recipients makes this view unlikely. Tax receipts are quite possible, with clans and villages sending commodities to appointed collectors.[37] Perhaps the ostraca are evidence for the tithe of 1 Sam 8:15 which went to royal officials. A problem is that the ostraca show that the same clan could send its commodities to more than one person (e.g., no. 35-39) and *vice versa*, a recipient could receive from more than one clan. This would have made for chaos in administration. If the chronological scheme suggested above is accepted, where approximately a generation separates the years 9-10 from years 15 and 17, then the problem of villages paying more than one person is largely overcome. Clans could send to more than one recipient (no. 35, 37) but individual village names are not given with them. If the village is the basic tax unit, then clans which occupy more than one village could conceivably owe commodities to more than one person; however, no village would owe commodities to more than one person.[38] This reconstruction depends on the village being the basic taxed unit even when not named in the clan ostraca, otherwise the logistical problem of multiple collectors and recipients for the same area still applies as negative evidence for this view.

(1962) 62-63; *Ibid.*, "The Samaria Ostraca in the Light of Fresh Evidence," *PEQ* 99 (1967) 32-41.

[36]   Treated in more depth by Lemaire (*Inscriptions*, 67-81).

[37]   As at Ugarit: see M. Heltzer, *The Rural Community in Ancient Ugarit* (Wiesbaden: Ludwig Reichert, 1976) 34. 39. In the Ugaritic texts silver taxes were collected by royal merchants and grain by overseers. Regional officials also collected taxes for the king in Neo-Assyria; cf. J. N. Postgate, *Taxation and Conscription*, 232-34.

[38]   Ostraca 13 and 21 may contradict this suggestion if one follows Aharoni's reading of the sherds in his *The Land of the Bible* (Philadelphia: Westminster Press, 1979) 360. Some individual letters are obscure and Lemaire (*Inscriptions*, 31-32) gives a different translation for no. 21.

(2)   Provisions for the royal palace. This interpretation has the advantage of stressing the most obvious fact about the ostraca: they are records of commodities received which were found in a storeroom near the royal palace. On this supposition, it is difficult to understand why so much information is recorded on most ostraca when a few ostraca record simply a date, a vineyard and a product (e.g., no. 20, 53-55, 60-61). These few ostraca probably are records of shipments to the royal palace but this conclusion leaves the purpose of the other ostraca still unanswered.[39]

(3)   Commodities from royal estates for servants and courtiers (officials) in the capital city. This interpretation has several supporters who differ only on a few details.[40]   To begin with, it has the general support of extra-biblical literature. Egypt,[41] Ugarit,[42] Alalakh,[43] and Assyria[44] have parallels consisting essentially of land grants from the royal estate to a recipient in return for the fulfillment of obligations. As apparently in Israel, a person is entitled to the land and its produce as a means of support including possible exemptions from such duties as taxation, conscription, *etc.*

The third interpretation is the most persuasive because it has the general support of cultural parallels, some evidence in the Hebrew Bible, and because the information recorded on most of the ostraca is consistent with this view. In concluding this, it must be acknowledged

---

[39]   Those ostraca with only the date, vineyard and product on them could hardly represent anything else but shipments to the royal palace; so Rainey ("Sitz im Leben,"92).

[40]   Lemaire, *Inscriptions*, 75-77.

[41]   *Ibid.*, 68-69.

[42]   *Ibid.*, 69-71; Rainey, "Administration in Ugarit," 62-63; Heltzer, *Rural Community*, 48-51, 103; M. Liverani, "Communautes de village et palais royal dans la Syrie du II eme millenaire," *JESHO* 18 (1975) 145-64.

[43]   D. J. Wiseman, "Alalakh," *Archaeology and Old Testament Study* (ed. D. W. Thomas; Oxford: The Clarendon Press, 1967) 124-29; H. Reviv, "Some Comments on the Maryannu," *IEJ* 22 (1972) 218-28. Reviv provides a detailed list of property and privileges extended to this class of aristocratic warriors by the king.

[44]   Postgate, *Royal Grants and Decrees*.

that some of the ostraca may record tax shipments as well which were intended for the same purpose of supporting recipients in Samaria. both the taxation of citizens and the produce from crown lands were necessary to support royal officials. If most of the ostraca do record deliveries from royal estates and land grants, some overlap between recipients is easily accounted for. As in the Ugaritic documents, people could be assigned a village, a field or vineyard, or several fields within a district.[45]   Indeed, it would be common for them as parts of former royal possessions to be near each other (cf. 2 Sam 14:30).

The case of Mephibosheth and his land grant is a good example of the way in which the system worked. As a patron of the royal court, he ate at the king's table but not at the king's expense. Ziba, Saul's former steward *(na'ar)*, was explicitly told to bring the produce in from the land so that Mephibosheth could eat (2 Sam 9:10). One can easily imagine what a receipt from the royal storehouse in Jerusalem would record.[46]

    A. In year 8
    B. from Gibeah (?)
    C. to *(1)* Meribaal (ben) Saul
    D. Ziba

The theory that the Samaria ostraca record shipments of commodities for the support of royal officials fits the evidence of the ostraca themselves and the parallels noted above. Not only is it the best and most plausible theory, it also allows for a possible rapprochement between the theories of tax receipts and shipments from land grants. The argument is usually made in terms of an exclusive option, either taxes or estate-shipments; however, the polemical speech in 1 Sam 8:11-17 seems to include the possibility of both in reference to the royal officials. In that passage, reference is made to fields granted to *(1)* the king's servants and to a commodities tax of a tenth levied on other landholdings which is also intended for their support. With this in mind, one must go further and ask who collected the taxes? Would it not have been the official to whom the commodities were due or, in certain cases, a peer also involved in royal service? Tax collection is an

---

45   Rainey, "The System of Land Grants," 187.
46   This suggestion and formulation was made by Rainey ("Sitz im Leben," 91-93).

important function for any bureaucracy; in Solomon's administration the head of the collection process for the provinces was a member of the "cabinet" (1 Kings 4:5) who had regional deputies working under him. In Nehemiah's administration there is mention of the officials *(seganīm)* involved with the collection of taxes and tithes and of the problems associated with the distribution of the produce to the intended recipients (Neh 12:44-45; 13:10-13. It is altogether likely that officials who collected taxes would receive the same support accorded other royal servants. The potential for graft and corruption would be enormous among officials for whom land grants and taxation were occupational privileges and who were partially supported by the taxes they collected.[47]   The nature of the ostraca make it unlikely that a firm distinction can be made among them between receipts for taxed commodities (perhaps years 9-10?) and those from land controlled by the recipients (years 15 and 17?). In fact, such a distinction may not have been important once the essential act of delivery had been accomplished.

Study of the place and clan names in the ostraca has also provided additional information on social structure in eighth-century Israel. Most of the names can be identified with modern Arab place names in a radius of a few miles around Samaria.[48]   The ostraca provide first-hand evidence from the eighth century of a rather densely populated region of small agricultural settlements in the hill country. In particular, the clan names demonstrate the continued existence of the village/clan social structure that evidently was still fundamental to Israelite society in spite of the preoccupation of many biblical writers (and modern scholars) with rulers and major cities. Samaria, and to a lesser degree regional cities such as Shechem, Tirzah and Dothan, were supported by the agricultural production of these smaller settlements in return for wich the cities provided regional administration and protection. The fact that these place names in the ostraca are known and recognized for administrative purposes by their clan names presupposes the continuance of the old agrarian patterns of close ties between the extended family and the land including the practice of family inheritance of property.

The ostraca, therefore, are valuable as illustrations of the fact that certain citizens received support while they resided in Samaria. We

---

[47]   *Supra.*, note 37.

[48]   Lemaire (*Inscriptions*, 55-65) has a discussion and map.

have concluded that they are evidence for the rights of officials in Samaria to hold land and receive support from its produce. Probably some ostraca are also receipts for tax shipments intended for the same purpose. The ostraca illustrate the type of social structure depicted in 1 Sam 8:11-17 and, in our assessment of the evidence, they provide insight into the type of property rights in conflict in the eighth century.

Judaean *lmlk* Stamps

Over one thousand jar handles stamped with *lmlk*, one of four place names in Judah, and a four or two winged disc design, have been discovered in Palestine.[49] Their discovery within ancient Judaean territory and their general date--eighth/seventh centuries--lead to the unanimous conclusion that they are associated with some facet of Judah's royal administration in the pre-exilic period.

Welten's published dissertation makes a lengthy review superfluous; however, a few remarks are necessary. Like the Samaria ostraca, the stamped handles are evidence for the crown's involvement in the shipment of commodities--again probably wine and oil--and for regional administrative work in at least the four places named: Hebron, Socah, Ziph, and *mmšt*.[50] Suggestions for the significance of the stamps include their use as royal measures, royal potteries, royal vineyards, or royal administrative centers.[51] The key for complete understanding would seem to lie with the significance of including one of these four place names on the stamp. Unfortunately for such analysis, no detailed excavation work has been done at any of the three known Judaean sites.[52] Nevertheless, important information has been gained from their discovery throughout Judaean territory.

Welten concluded that the place names referred to royal land holdings which produced commodities for the king's use. The fact that Hebron, Socoh and Ziph are not mentioned as major cities during the

---

[49]   P. Welten, *Die Königs-Stempel* (Wiesbaden: Otto Harrassowitz, 1969).

[50]   *Ibid.*, 147-56, on the possible locations for this place.

[51]   Y. Yadin, "The Fourfold Division of Judah," *BASOR* 163 (1961) 6-12, suggests that the four place names indicate Judah's division into four regions for defense and ease of supply and delivery provisions.

[52]   The work of P. C. Hammond at Hebron, *RB* 73 (1966) 566-69; *RB* 75 (1968) 253-56, is of little assistance in the present discussion.

eighth century, and *mmšt* not at all, is explained by him as understandable because their primary significance must have been as part of the royal estate.[53]   The three known sites are mentioned by the Chronicler as places fortified by Rehoboam (2 Chron 11;7, 8, 10). Welten considered this fact, along with the wide distribution of handles throughout Judaean territory, as evidence ror his conclusion that the stamped jars contained supplies for military units during the reigns of Hezekiah and Josiah.

Since Welten's work the renewed excavations at *Tell ed Duweir* have contributed the information that both the 4-winged design and the 2-winged one were found together in the same stratum (III), whereas Welten had attributed the two types to Hezekiah (4-winged) and to Josiah (2-winged) respectively. If stratum III was destroyed ca 701 B.C.E., as the current excavators have concluded,[54] then both designs were in use during Hezekiah's reign.[55] It is not yet clear whether the winged designs were discontinued after his reign or continued in use under Josiah, but at some point before 587/86 a rosetta design on jar handles was adopted for official use.[56]

An eighth century date for the *lmlk* stamps makes them an important contemporary witness for the widespread nature of the royal administration and to the territory under Judaean control. Welten's conclusion about the stamped jars as containing supplies for the military is probable because it accounts for their wide distribution in fortified cities or fortresses.[57] The geographical distribution of the stamps fit what can be reconstructed for Hezekiah's reign and military

---

53   Welten (*Die Königs-Stempel*, 141-42) answers the question of why only four place names are used with, "dass die Erträge der vier Krongüter (wenigstens zu einem Teil) für einen bestimmten Zweck aus dem übrigen Krongutsertrag ausgeschieden wurden."

54   D. Ussishkin, "The Destruction of Lachish by Sennacherib and the Dating of the Royal Judaen Storage Jars," *TA* 4 (1977) 28-60.

55   H. D. Lance, "Royal Stamps and the Kingdom of Judah," *HTR* 72 (1971) 315-32, had argued that the two designs were in use simultaneously but insisted the stamps date to Josiah's reign.

56   *Land of the Bible*, 400.

57   Only Beth Shemesh of the sites where the seals have so far been discovered seems to have been unfortified during this period.

strategy better than that of Josiah.[58]   Also, in the record of Hezekiah's building projects are specific references to storehouses (2 Kings 20:13; 2 Chron 32:27-29).   The four cities inscribed on the stamps could be among his cities or storehouses, part of his royal estate that produced the commodities, or royal centers for pottery craftsmen.   Perhaps a combination of regional storehouses and pottery centers[59] best fits the available evidence.   It is difficult to imagine, however, why the location of the site producing the commodities would be important for inclusion on the stamp; furthermore, it seems likely that the contents of the jars would have come from various sources such as taxes, tariffs and booty as well as from the king's royal estate.

The *lmlk* stamps, therefore, are good contemporary evidence for the distribution of royally designated supplies.   They indirectly point to a substantial state and regional administration which would be required to maintain the distributing system.   The stamps are also indirect evidence for the existence of royal estates and taxes, both of which would be necessary for supplying the commodities for distribution.

Excavations in Palestine have produced a large number of other seals and seal impressions containing a personal name and/or a title. The vast majority of these seals date to the eighth-seventh centuries.[60] Their function is that of providing proof of ownership for the material stamped, whether it be the wax sealing of a document or a jar handle. Private citizens could possess these seals, at least this is the common view of those seals lacking a title.   The titles so far discovered *(e.g.,*

---

[58]   N. Na'aman, "Sennacherib's Campaign to Judah and the date of the '*lmlk*' stamps," *VT* 29 (1979) 71-86, has shown that the spread of the seals relates much better to what can be reconstructed for Hezekiah's reign than for Josiah's.   This fact was a link in Lance's discussion, *supra*, note 55.

[59]   P. Lapp, "Late Royal Seals from Judah," *BASOR* 158 (1960) 14-16, states that of all the seal impressions he examined, all could have been made with only a few seals.   This implies the jars were made in a small number of potteries.

[60]   A translation and bibliography for nearly every published seal (impression) can be found in L. G. Herr, *The Scripts of Ancient North-West Semitic Seals* (HDR 18, Missoula: Scholars Press, 1978).

naᶜar, ᶜebed, ben melek, ᶜal habāyit) represent officials of the king, their servants, and perhaps other public functionaries.[61]

These seals and seal impressions are important for two reasons. (1) They provide evidence for a rise in a type of commerce and bureaucracy that required such seals for the protection and maintenance of property rights and a guarantee of origin. (2) The titled seals are evidence for the presence of public functionaries in both kingdoms of the eighth century and reflect something of their importance and growing influence on commerce of the period.

Summary and Conclusions

The evidence discussed in this chapter leads to the conclusion that certain rights of the king to grant land and tax support to his officials provides a completely plausible and consistent background to the prophetic accusations over property rights. Two of the most prominent factors in the prophetic critique, i.e., *land appropriation and exactions of various kinds*, can be traced to the exercise of rights granted by the crown to its appointees. The fact that several of the prophetic accusations name or imply officials who are involved in these practices is what one would expect if the land-grant system for patronage was a prominent contributor to the perceived social problems. The social and economic imbalance created by this system seems inevitable.

It must be admitted, however, that different types of evidence have been mixed to arrive at these conclusions. The parody of 1 Sam 8:11-17 can be assessed differently; while we see in the passage evidence for the bitterness of some property owners over the curtailment of what they perceive as their rights of possession, others view the passage as late and historically suspect or as a reference to the practices of non-Israelite kingship. In our view the practices that are parodied are seen as further evidence for the circumstances of perceived oppression in the eighth century prophets. This is a logical and plausible conclusion (and probable!), but it requires the comparison of two different types of evidence and is by no means a necessary conclusion.

The use of epigraphic remains to illustrate the functioning systems of land grants, taxation, and the influence of the royal administration is

---

61   N. Avigad, "New Light on the Naᶜar Seals," *Magnalia Dei* (ed. F. M. Cross, *et al.*; Garden City: Doubleday, 1976) 294-300, provides bibliography and a discussion of the function of some titled seal-holders.

yet a third type of evidence. The material seems illuminating for the thesis, but its fragmentary nature is always suspect for a comprehensive solution. Were biblical scholars to have administrative and legal documents at their disposal from ancient Israel like those discovered at Ugarit or Mari, undoubtedly more detailed information and insight could be gained. The cuneiform materials from the Neo-Assyrian empire briefly discussed in Excursus Two clearly demonstrates how helpful these kinds of documents can be. In fact, the types of socio-economic relationships we have proposed for eighth-century Israel and Judah find several striking parallels in the Neo-Assyrian material. The parallels include the rights of officials to land and taxes, with a corresponding rise in landed estates and indebtedness among other segments of society.

In this chapter there are points of agreement and disagreement with the influential views of Alt and his students. As noted in previous discussion, Alt correctly recognized the prominent role of officials in the prophetic accusations and attributed this fact to the new economic and cultural circumstances under kingship. He minimized, however, the value of 1 Sam 8:11-17[62] for understanding this phenomenon and placed most of his emphasis on the view that Canaanite social practices were replacing older Israelite customs. As we have seen in this chapter and elsewhere, this reconstruction of Canaanite predominance in socio-economic practice cannot be substantiated. The practices parodied in 1 Sam 8:11-17 are not specifically Canaanite nor, when understood as references to land grants, taxation and conscription, expressly forbidden in the Hebrew Bible.

---

[62]   Alt, "Der Anteil," 356-58.

Excursus Two

Neo-Assyrian Administrative Practices

Recent publications have hrought to light several aspects of administrative practices and the inner workings of the Neo-Assyrian empire.[63]   These published texts were uncovered during the Nimrud excavations conducted by the British School of Archaeology in Iraq and have been securely dated by Assyrian synchronisms. Most texts date to the first half of the eighth century but a few are ninth or seventh century in origin. Nimrud, or ancient *Kalḫu* was the Assyrian capital built by Assurnasirpal (883-859). In addition to the royal palace, the site also contained a provincial governor's palace with archives.

In the notes to the previous chapters there are several references to proposed cultural similarities or parallels between Neo-Assyrian practices and those in Israel or Judah. Several of these similarities are again noted in this excursus along with others not previously mentioned. The list is limited to those practices we have insisted are fundamental for the understanding of issues over property in the eighth-century prophets. A much larger list could be compiled because the value of these texts for comparison with Israelite practices has been generally overlooked.

(1) Provincial Administration. Even before Tiglath-Pileser's administrative reorganization in the third quarter of the eighth century, the expanding Neo-Assyrian empire had an extensive provincial system staffed by influential families with appointed royal authority. Various titles *(bēl piḫati, šaknu, rab ālāni)* are recorded for these administrators.[64] Their administrative/judicial duties included military leadership, the levy and the collection of rations for government use. Regarding this last duty, Kinnier Wilson concluded that the governor had two major responsibilities: "to supply his own household (several

---

63   J. N. Postgate, *The Governor's Palace Archive* (London: The British School of Archaeology, 1973);   *Ibid., Taxation and Conscription; Ibid., Royal Grants and Decrees;* J. V. Kinnier Wilson, *The Nimrud Wine Lists. A Study of Men and Administration at the Assyrian Capital in the Eighth Century, B. C.* (London: The British School of Archaeology, 1973).

64   Kinnier Wilson, *Wine Lists*, 12-18.

clues suggest that this may often have been sizeable), and to make available the supply to the king's household."[65]

(2)   Land Grants.   The Neo-Assyrian kings made frequent use of this right.[66]   Like most kings in the ancient Near East, the Assyrian monarchs controlled or claimed ownership of vast territories and used this property to reward their servants. Exemptions from service or taxation sometimes went with these grants.[67]   In some cases the documents show that the grants from the king were a basis for his servants in building bigger estates for themselves, including property in provinces other than the one in which they served.

(3)   Taxation and Conscription. The Neo-Assyrian empire regularly collected taxes (usually in kind) from internal provinces.[68] Postgate concluded in his study that even under the lucrative reign of Esarhaddon the regular taxation of internal provinces produced more wealth for the empire than did tribute from vassals.[69]   The provincial governments were responsible for implementing taxation and conscription policies determiined by the central government. Taxes were collected by regional officials[70]   and stored in fortified cities. Taxes in kind were regularly exacted based on an ideal production rate, and flocks were subject to royal taxation as well.   Labor was conscripted by the authority of the central government and directed by royal servants in the provinces. The army contained a professional nucleus which was supplemented by conscripted troops.

(4)   Officers as Creditors. The governor's palace texts contained several receipts (no. 90-99) that show officials paying or assuming the debts of others. Three of these texts show the provincial governor, *Bēl-tarṣi-iluma* (*ca* 800 B. C. E.), assuming the obligations of citizens' debts. The receipts are evidence that the debtors owe nothing to former

---

65   *Ibid.*, 15.
66   Postgate, *Neo-Assyrian Royal Grants and Decrees.*
67   *Ibid.*, 9-16, for a list of exemptions and privileges.
68   Postgate, *Taxation and Conscription.*
69   *Ibid.*, 216-217.
70   Kinnier Wilson, *Wine Lists*, 15-18.

creditors but are now indebted to the governor.[71]   Such agreements *could* lead to further property acquisitions by these officials.

Three officials known from the palace archives illustrate practices employed to acquire property. The first, *Bēl-issīya,* was a village inspector and a eunuch of the governor. During his thirty-five year career he was involved in at least seven sales texts and in three others he was a contracting party. He also served as a creditor to private citizens.[72]   The second, *Sîn-ēṭir,* was a brother and official of the governor. He also purchased several tracts of land, some of which lay at a considerable distance from the capital. One text (no. 64) has him simply exchanging land with another citizen demonstrating that his transactions were for his private benefit even though the contracts were preserved in official archives.[73]   The third, *Šamaš-kumua,* was a scribe and eunuch of the palace who made multiple land purchases.[74]

According to Postgate, these three officials are examples who show that "not only the highest officials and provincial governors were able to acquire estates in separate provinces at the time of Adad-Nirari III."[75] Other scholars have observed that administrative practices by officials in the empire led to the rise of landed estates controlled by these officials.[76]   Differences remain, however, concerning the interpretation of this fact. One view has it that conditions in the provincial countryside had deteriorated so badly that the original village communities had become "slave communities, devoted to production on

---

[71]   Postgate, *Palace Archive,* 17. He believes the receipts show the beginnings of a governmental policy intended for the protection of creditors. It is debatable whether the protection of creditors was the primary goal; perhaps the acquisition of the debtor and his/her property was also in the governor's mind.

[72]   *Ibid.,* 12-13; texts 15-16, 33-35, 94.

[73]   *Ibid.,* 14; texts 20, 64-65, and probably 37, 42, 47.

[74]   *Ibid.,* 14-15; texts 17, 31.

[75]   *Ibid.,* 13.

[76]   F. M. Fales, *Censimenti e catasti di epica neoassira* (Studi economici e technologici 2; Rome: University of Rome, 1973); G. van Driel, "Land and People in Assyria," *BiOr* 27 (1970) 168-75.

behalf of the officials, in an extensive series of adjacent lots."[77]   A more moderate assessment comes from van Driel: "the rights of the individual subject were limited and circumscribed by a whole range of circumstances, of which the ownership of land and the rights of the government are only the most crucial."[78]

However the Assyrian evidence is assessed, the similarities between it and the circumstances reconstructed for Israel and Judah are obvious. The importance of the Assyrian evidence is not just chronological proximity but the administrative documents which provide the documentary connection between the landed estates, taxation, and indebtedness which we have proposed for Israel and Judah on the basis of non-administrative texts.[79]

The similarity between some Neo-Assyrian administrative practices and those in Israel or Judah raise the question of actual influence or simple cultural parallels. This question cannot be answered from the material presented in this excursus. Scholars have traditionally looked to Egypt or the Canaanite city-states for influence in Israel or Judah. There is enough evidence in the Neo-Assyrian material to question whether either of these cultures had the decisive influence upon Israel or Judah often assumed.[80]

---

[77]   Fales *Censimenti*, 131. The translation is provided by J. N. Postgate in his "Some Remarks on Conditions in the Assyrian Countryside," *JESHO* 17 (1974) 231.

[78]   Van Driel, "Land and People," 174.

[79]   There are other points of interest for biblical scholars in the administrative documents of the Neo-Assyrian archive such as Kinner Wilson's suggestion (*Nimrud Wine Lists*, 95-98) of triangles of administration in the empire. By this he means a head, a lieutenant, and a scribe for all major governmental institutions. He compares 2 Kings 19:2 which presupposes the triangle of *melek*, *ᶜal habbāyit*, and *hassōpēr*.

[80]   The competent work of Mettinger *(Solomonic State Officials)* does not discuss the possible influence of Neo-Assyrian bureaucracy upon civil government in Israel or Judah.

Chapter Five

Backgrounds to the Conflict over Property Rights

In the previous chapters the prophetic accusations over the perceived loss of property rights were analyzed and interpreted as a result of internal policies in both Judah and Israel. The purpose of this chapter is to offer answers to the following questions: why did the prophetic protests occur in the eighth century; and specifically, what influential factors contributed to their protests over issues of property? The proposed answers can only be partial. There are, however, certain socio-economic and historical factors which can be suggested as primary influences. This discussion shall be made under two headings: internal developments and external influences.

Internal Developments

As noted in the Introduction, many scholars concluded that internal developments within Israel and Judah led to the prophetic protests. Under the monarchy, rising commercialism, a developing "money" economy, icreased trade, etc., resulted in a bifurcaction in society and relatively rapid social change. Such developments often resulted in protests over the growth of a proletariat and the perception that traditional values were being displaced. In popular reconstruction, the prophets reacted against the fact that the rich became richer and the poor more destitute; or similarly, they protested against a capitalistic society where wealth was concentrated in the hands of a few wealthy citizens.

One cannot deny the element of truth contained in such a reconstruction. The sociologist J. R. Rosenbloom has shown how the rapid growth under David and Solomon is a classic illustration of the tensions between centralization and decentralization and of the nation-builders who "over-reach and overspend."[1]   Indeed, the two hundred and fifty years between Saul, the first king, and Amos saw several points of social tension including Absalom's rebellion, the division of

---

[1]   J. R. Rosenbloom, "Social Science Concepts of Modernization and Biblical History: The Development of the Israelite Monarchy," *JAAR* 40 (1972) 437-444, esp. 444.

the nation, and Jehu's *coup.* In one sense, the prophetic protests reflect years of socio-economic, political, and religious tensions.

On the other hand, the preceding investigation suggests certain refinements must be made in this view--at least with regard to the conflict over property rights. For example, the accusations concerning property rights presuppose that the anonymous rich and powerful of popular reconstruction are often officials or royal servants who are reaping benefits from their positions. The rights accorded royal servants such as land grants and taxation privileges were primary factors in building landed estates and a corresponding increase in the personal indebtedness of ordinary citizens.

These circumstances are also reasons for concluding that the propensity to describe the Israelite economy as "capitalistic" is misguided and inaccurate. As noted in the Introduction, there is little evidence of a large private market in Israel or Judah, which is indispensable for a capitalistic economy. Instead, the land grant and patronage systems are examples of the state's influence upon the economy, and it is more likely that state policies in Israel and Judah had a more determining role in the use of the economy's surplus than did the manipulation of supply and demand by private entrepreneurs. An archaeologist has reached essentially the same conclusion about state policy in eighth century Judah by using anthropological data and systems theory. McClellan's study concluded:

> The urban settlements of 8th century B. C. Judah reveal that there was a high degree of specialization by various towns and groups within towns; they were integrated into a regional network in which their surpluses were redistributed. The economic system was organized by the state, under the leadership of the king in his administrative center, Jerusalem...The public works involved in the construction of the city defenses, water systems, and storehouses, and the distribution of the storage jars with *lmlk* stamp seals, however they were used, seem to be too highly organized to be other than centralized enterprises of the king.[2]

---

[2]   T. McClellan, "Towns and "Fortresses: The transformation of Urban Life in Judah from 8th to 7th Centuries B. C.," *SBLSP* (Missoula: Scholars Press, 1978) 1. 281. Similar judgments could be made about Israel's socio-economic structure in the eighth century before the fall of Samaria.

The key term used by McClellan is "redistributed," for it describes well the function of land grants and taxation privileges where property is (re)distributed by royal policies. The term *redistribution system* is, in fact, the phrase used by some analysts to describe a common form of economy in antiquity developed under monarchy.[3] While virtually all economies redistribute goods and services, this description is used particularly to identify an economy in antiquity which had a monarch or strong, central leader who developed trading relations with other nations and who required loyal servants for assistance in co-ordinating redistributing mechanisms.   Carney, for example, states that bureaucracies in antiquity usually developed from the redistribution economy because of the need for skilled servants and capable officials. Such bureauracracies were usually regulative and extractive, not developmental, and "most of any society's tiny elite went into the apparatus of the government."[4] The ruler frequently used patronage to ensure the loyalty of the subordinates. As Carney defines the function of patronage in a redistributing economy, it "provides subordinates who can be utterly relied upon by superiors and vice versa...It perverts the legal process, due process, the operation of the market, bureaucratic ethics and what have you."[5] By this last statement he means there is a tendency to treat citizens as subjects who have "little security against official power and with little in the way of <u>property rights</u>"[6](my emphasis, J.A.D.).

These observations about a particular type of economy in antiquity provide persuasive insights in support of conclusions reached in the earlier chapters.   Other terms such as *Frühkapitalismus* or even *Rentenkapitalismus* are less helpful and, on occasion, one suspects such terms are used with modern analogies in mind. A redistributing economy is a better description for Israel and Judah under monarchy. The crucial role of the state in redistributing substantial segments of the economy's production is important for understanding the place of land grants, taxation privileges, and patronage in the conflict over property rights in the eighth century.

---

3   Carney, *The Economics of Antiquity*, 21-22, 36, 64-70; Nash, *Primitive and Peasant Economic Systems*, 26-33.

4   Carney, *Economics*, 36.

5   *Ibid.*, 64-65.

6   *Ibid.*, 69.

The characteristics of a redistributing economy also provide insight into individual conclusions reached in previous chapters. (1) The sociological assumption that much of any ancient society's elite had a role in the apparatus of government corresponds well with the conclusion from Chapters One, Three and Four, that many of those responsible for the perceived schemes were officials of various types. (2) Carney's observation of a tendency to treat citizens more like subjects (and thus with far fewer property rights) appears to be an accurate description of the conflict between the rights of officials and those of citizens proposed for the eighth century in Israel and Judah. This observation also accounts for the perceived success of the oppression and its *legality*. (3) Carney's negative judgment on patronage and its effects describes almost exactly the earlier conclusion reached about conflicts within the land grant system of patronage.

It must be admitted, however, that there is a danger of prejudice in this analysis. It cannot be assumed automatically that kings and royal officials initiated policies designed for graft and corruption, or solely for the maximizing of revenue. For example, the investigation of the administrative/judicial system concluded that a type of bi-level, state organization had developed by the eighth century whose authority often overshadowed the local assembly of elders. Such a system can be understood from a perspective which wanted a judicial reform and more consistency (cf. 1 Sam 8:1-3). The fact that the state system seems to have fallen prey to corruption and graft does nothing to negate these intentions. Similarly, many actions undertaken in a redistributing economy were probably enacted for laudable reasons such as national security.[7]

Most of the practices suggested for understanding the eighth-century protests existed before that century. One developing factor was the more centralized state, administrative/judicial system which does not seem to have been implemented until the ninth (Jehoshaphat?) or perhaps the eighth century. If there were any newer influences which contributed to the eighth century prophetic protests, then external factors are the likely source.

---

[7]   Crüsemann *(Der Widerstand)* surveys the variety of opinions toward kingship in the Hebrew Bible, noting the range between positive and negative assessments.

External Influences

The primary external influence upon internal policies in Israel or Judah was the force of international relations. The rapid rise of the Davidic/Solomonic state took place in a virtual political vacuum where the influence of Egypt or Mesopotamia was minimal. For centuries before and after, however, this was not the case. More typically, internal developments reflected the influence of larger political relationships.

In Israel and Judah internal socio-economic developments did not evolve unhindered but were often a consequence of larger political relationships. For example, the Omride Dynasty in Israel turned a stable relationship with several of its neighbors into a very lucrative empire.[8] Ahab solidified relations with his Sidonian counterpart through marriage and evidently had good relations with his Judaean counterpart as well. The choice of Samaria as a royal and international city is evidence of the dynasty's progressive outlook. Perhaps the most revealing indication of the dynasty's importance is the prominent role it played in the Qarqar coalition which met the Assyrian army in 853. As Tadmor has emphasized, this coalition was economically motivated and represented a solid opposition to the Assyrian attempt to control trading routes in Syria/Palestine.[9] The coalition was a rare display of cooperation among the nations of the area and perhaps helps explain the prosperity in evidence for the Omride dynasty.

It was not long before the fragile coalition disintegrated and the fortunes of Israel plummeted in the second half of the ninth century. Moab revolted against Israelite hegemony[10] and Jehu overthrew the Omrides in reaction to their international and syncretistic policies. A dynasty change in Damascus brought Hazael to the throne along with

---

8   J. M. Miller, *The Omride Dynasty in the Light of Recent Literary and Archaeological Research* (unpublished dissertation; Emory University, 1964).

9   H. Tadmor, "Assyria and the West: The Ninth Century and its Aftermath," *Unity and Diversity. Essays in the History, Literature, and Religion of the Ancient Near East* (ed. H. Goedicke and J. J. M. Roberts; Baltimore: Johns Hopkins, 1975) 39.

10   Moabite Stone, *ANET*, 320.

renewed Aramaean might.[11] Shalmaneser III campaigned in the west in 841, severely attacking Hazael although without receiving tribute, and humbling Jehu as well.[12] Jehu's bloodletting had cut ties with the Phoenicians and the Judaeans. His payment of tribute, however, made him an unwilling vassal of Assyria and prey for Aramaean ambitions. After Shalmaneser's campaign, an alliance of Aramaean states led by Hazael reached the peak of its power and dominated the west through most of the century. Israel is portrayed as humiliated, like the dust at threshing, and with almost no army (2 Kings 13:7). Moreover, Hazael took control of Transjordanian territory claimed by Israel (2 Kings 10: 32-33). Judah's fortunes at this time were similar to Israel's. Hazael moved down the Philistine coast and took Gath (*T. es Safi?*), and prepared to assault Jerusalem. Judah's king, Joash, then gathered tribute to deter Hazael from an actual siege (2 Kings 12: 18-19).

The point of this survey relates to the economic fortunes of Israel and Judah. While David and Solomon took advantage of a temporary lull in power politics to build an empire, the historic powers in the ancient Near East made it inevitable that the anomaly of an Israelite empire would not last. No fragile empire or coalition in Syria/Palestine could survive the pressure of Assyrian might when neighbors (such as Damascus) had designs of their own. Israel's decline meant the loss of lucrative trading ventures with both northern and southern neighbors so that much of the economic surplus generated by commerce was lost to Aramaean hegemony. This would seem especially true in the loss of the Transjordanian territory where trading routes and tribute must have been profitable to the Omrides. There is nothing to suggest that the more isolated Judah fared any better.

In 806 (and probably 796)[13] the Assyrians under Adad-nirari III turned westward to meet the Aramaean coalition under the leadership of Damascus. The Aramaeans were a formidable opposition to Assyrian desires for westward expansion. Damascus and the Aramaeans received a devastating blow which, while not extinguishing hopes for

---

[11]   A. Malamat, "The Aramaeans," *Peoples of Old Testament Times* (ed. D. J. Wiseman; Oxford: The Clarendon Press, 1973) 134-55, esp. 144-45.

[12]   *ANET*, 280; M. Astour, "The First Assyrian Invasion of Israel," *JAOS* 91 (1971) 383-89.

[13]   *ANET*, 281; H. Tadmor and A. R. Millard, "Adad Nirari III in Syria," *Iraq* 35 (1973) 57-65.

resurgence, did loosen the stranglehold on Israel (Judah too?) and forced the center of Aramaean influence to move northward to Hamath. Israel also paid tribute to the Assyrians at this time.[14]

There are several important considerations which arise from this turn of events. One is that Israel and Judah began slowly to recover and subsequently to reassert old claims to empire. A second is that Assyria was now preoccupied with a trade axis in the north and west of Palestine that seemed to stifle its imperialistic interests. A study on Phoenician trading patterns and pottery distribution concludes that an Assyrian *decline* from ca. 824-744 was a consequence of a North Syrian-Urartian alliance.[15] Urartu was at the heighth of its power[16] and had good relations with Elam in the east resulting in control of the eastern trade routes. Good relations between the North Syrian states and Urartu effectively controlled the northern and western routes as well and threatened to shut Assyria out. Frankenstein concludes that "the full economic resurgence of Assyria in the late eighth century depended essentially on the destruction of the North Syrian-Urartian alliance in the north and west."[17] She has made a persuasive case for her conclusion, perhaps with the one qualification that Assyrian *decline* was not so much a sign of weakness as evidence for the tenacity and effectivenss of the alliance. A third consideration is the relationship of Israel to Assyria since Jehu's *coup*. Almost since its inception, the Jehu dynasty had a vassal relationship with Assyria and had provided tribute more than once to the king. Some scholars have seen Jehu's capitulation to Shalmaneser in 841 as acceptance of Assyrian protection and possibly a stamp of legitimacy for his rule.[18] Others suggest that Adad-nirari III's later lenient treatment of Israel--as distinguished from the treatment of Damascus--resulted from the Assyrian desire to

---

14   *Supra.*, note 13, for the Assyrian texts.

15   S. Frankenstein, "The Phoenicians in the Far West: A Function of Neo-Assyrian Imperialism," *Power and Propaganda. A Symposium on Ancient Empires* (Mesopotamia 7; ed. M. Trolle Larsen; Copenhagen: Akademisk Forlag, 1979) 263-94.

16   A. Goetze, *Kleinasien* (KAO III/1; München: Beck, 1957) 187-200.

17   Frankenstein, "Phoenicians," 271.

18   Tadmor, "Assyria and the West," 40; Astour, "The First Assyrian Invasion," 383-89; E. Lipinski, "An Assyro-Israelite Alliance in 842/41 B.C.E.," *Sixth World Congress of Jewish Studies, 1.* 273-78.

maintain a nominal vassalship with Israel while encouraging the nation to be independent from and opposed to Aramaean domination.[19] Frankenstein's study provides a good reason why Assyria would seek ties with Israel; the latter was a western state near the trading routes with little regard for the Aramaeans.

With Assyria struggling for power elsewhere, the states of Israel and Judah began the road to political and economic recovery. This, of course, is the immediate background to the accusations of the eighth century prophets concerning property rights. During the first half of the eighth century, both states expanded during this temporary lull in the area. Israel seems to have taken advantage of the temporary power vacuum by forced expansion. The king most closely associated with this recovery in 2 Kings is Jeroboam II.

Israel

The actual territory controlled by Jeroboam is disputed.[20] It is recorded that he "restored the border of Israel from Lebo-Hamath as far as the Sea of the Arabah" (2 Kings 14:25). This statement is to be compared to Amos 6:13-14 where, after a punning satire on the taking of Lo-Debar and Karnaim, the prophet predicts oppression for Israel "from Lebo-Hamath to the brook of the Arabah." This Amos text is not necessarily a description of Israel's borders at that time, but perhaps only a reference to well known geographical places or the traditional pan-Israel ideal. Furthermore, Jeroboam's acquisition of territory was not accomplished all at once. According to 2 Kings 14:28, Jeroboam took Damascus and Hamath, but this is probably a secondary tradition since Damascus appears in Amos 1:3-5 as a power to be broken. The most probable situation is that Jeroboam reasserted nominal control over the Transjordanian trade routes (i.e., the King's Highway) from northern Moab into Aramaean territory, taking up a role the Aramaeans had assumed in the latter part of the ninth century.

Israel's recovery began with reduced territory and the nation at a low ebb. Its expansion achieved limited success because Assyrian interests lay farther north. And the wealth and power of Jeroboam's kingdom have been overestimated; it is likely that only the court and its officials

---

19   Tadmor and Millard, "Adad Nirari III," 65.

20   M. Haran, "The Rise and Decline of the Empire of Jeroboam ben Joash," *VT* 17 (1967) 267-84.

were well-to-do in this period. His rapid rebuilding policies[21] seem to have produced circumstances lamented by Amos just as similar policies produced discontent earlier under Solomon and Rehoboam. There seems to be an important difference between the policies of the Omrides and those of Jeroboam II. The Omrides secured some lucrative ventures through intermarriage and trade agreements while Jeroboam II took advantage of a temporary power vacuum in the area with forced expansion.

This reconstruction of political events requires correlation with previous conclusions about internal developments in Israel. Amos' perception of an economically divided state is understandable. After repeated payment of tribute and recent Aramaean domination, condidtions could not have been very good for the average citizen. The oppressive lifestyle of the rich which Amos opposed was probably the habit of a few who were closely associated with the royal court. Certainly the attempt to rebuild an army and expand control over Transjordan required taxation, a loyal cadre of servants, and a firm rule by the king. A crucial point is this addition of the broader context to the previously provided reconstructions of internal administrative practices. Conflict in the social realm would seem inevitable. Any state which was recovering from an economic and political decline, but which redistributed most of the economy's surplus among its own officials, would be ripe for protest. A socio-economic structure with a propensity for imbalance would become so through the pressure of external circumstances such as repeated requirements for tribute and the cost of military defeat.

The issue of Neo-Assyrian influence has been raised from the standpoint of both internal, administrative practices and external political relations. Regarding the latter, it does seem certain that Israel had political relations with Assyria from 841 on, and it seems probable that Assyria encouraged these relations out of its own self interest in opposing the Aramaeans. An important aspect of Amos' prophecy appears to be related to this conclusion. It concerns his knowledge of and interest in political relations in Syria-Palestine. His perception that historical destruction would come and that captivity and exile would

---

21   Cf. A. Biran, "Tel Dan--5 Years Later," *BA* 43 (1980) 168-82, esp. 176-77; A. Ben Tor, "Excavations at Tel Yokneam," *IEJ* 29 (1979) 83; K. Kenyon, *Archaeology in the Holy Land* (New York: W. Norton, 1979) 335, on Megiddo; S. Geva, "A Reassessment of the Chronology of Beth Shean Stratum V and IV," *IEJ* 29 (1979) 6-10.

follow is simply a reflection of Assyrian practices. Even his emphasis on national, corporate punishment could be derived from knowledge of Assyrian custom.[22]

The issue of Assyrian influence on Israelite administrative practice is a difficult one. Excursus Two provides several specific instances where Neo-Assyrian practices parallel those reconstructed for Israel. This correspondence appears to exist on a more fundamental level as well. Several scholars have pointed out that the Neo-Assyrian empire fell prey to an imperialist pattern where the center of the empire became a parasite on the periphery.[23] The rich and politically elite owned estates in the provinces where their influence was manifest in controlling much of the administrative/judicial processes, agricultural production, and tax collection. The accumulation of wealth in the capital and key provincial cities led to instability and finally collapse of the empire.[24]

Neo-Assyria had developed the most efficient administrative system in the ancient Near East of its day. It is entirely conceivable that Israel adopted--or better, adapted--some of their own administrative methods from Assyria, particularly if the Jehu dynasty received the attention from Assyria previously proposed. Both Samaria and *Kalḫu* became new capital cities in the ninth century and, as Mallowan has pointed out, were cities with a surprisingly similar culture.[25] Even the

---

[22]   J. S. Holladay, "Assyrian Statecraft and the Prophets of Israel," *HTR* 63 (1970) 29-51.

[23]   Postgate, "The Economic Structure of the Assyrian Empire," 193-221.

[24]   *Ibid.*, 217-21. In his *Taxation and Conscription*, 201-02, Postgate concludes that the extraction of wealth from the countryside into the capital and provincial cities led to a concentration of wealth in the hands of officials, merchants and usurers. Unstable conditions developing in the countryside in seemingly prosperous times resulted in the collapse of the nation's strength. We are proposing a similar set of circumstances for Israel of the eighth century.

[25]   M. Mallowan, "Samaria and Calah-Nimrud: Conjunctions in History and Archaeology," *Archaeology in the Levant. Essays for Kathleen Kenyon* (ed. R. Moorey and P. Parr; Warminster: Aris & Phillips, 1978). 155-63.

military structure of armies in the west may have been influenced by Assyrian administration.[26]

As noted in previous chapters, the spectre of Canaanite influence and customs is often posited as the key to the conflict over property rights in Israel. Whether there was substantial Neo-Assyrian influence or not, the fact that substantial parallels do exist lessens the probability of an already weak Canaanite hypothesis. To defend this hypothesis, one needs to explain how the Jehu dynasty, which is depicted as virulent in its opposition to Canaanite influence, was the dynasty responsible for implementing (or continuing) such practices. It is much more likely that these practices of land grants, land alienation, and taxation privileges were considered acceptable Israelite practices just as they seem in other cultures of the ancient Near East.

Finally, the Syro-Ephraimite alliance (Isa 7:1-2) was an attempted return to the coalition of the previous century. There can be little doubt that Damascus under Rezin was the ringleader and they were punished accordingly by Assyria. Some national leaders obviously wished to folow the lead of Damascus and at least Hoshea, the appointed king of Samaria, followed the lead of Assyria.[27] Any discussion of a pro-Canaanite party or platform in Israel will not only have difficulty defining Canaanite, but will also need to account for the more obvious pro-Aramaean and pro-Assyrian interest groups known from the Assyrian inscriptions and the Hebrew Bible.

Judah

The Judaean king Azariah/Uzziah, with his son Jotham as vice-regent (2 Kings 15:5), was a vigorous ruler. He was a contemporary of Jeroboam II and during this time Judah's resurgence paralleled that of Israel. Uzziah attempted to gain control of southern Transjordan by rebuilding Elath (2 Kings 14:22). Perhaps he also expanded westward to defeat the Philistines and southward to control the Arab tribes (2 Chron 26:6-7). His eastward expansion is said to have reached the

---

26   Cf. 1 Kings 20:24, where the Aramaean military leader commands that the petty kings be replaced by *paḥôt*, commanders. The word may be an Aramaism, as it occurs several times in post-exilic writings, but its cognate is the standard title for an Assyrian provincial governor, a *(bēl) piḥati.*

27   *ANET*, 284.

Ammonites who were forced to pay him tribute. His intent seems clear: to control the trading routes and highways in these three areas.[28] Moreover, it is recorded that he built cities and fortresses, conducted a census,[29] and possessed much personal property (2 Chron 26:9-15).

It is improbable that Uzziah led a coalition of states against the Assyrians as sometimes proposed.[30] Judah, however, did help fill the power gap in Palestine caused by the decline of the Aramaean coalition and Assyrian neglect. Thus Judah and Israel together held at least nominal control over territory nearly the size of the former united monarchy.

The fortunes of Judah changed from that of Israel in the third quarter of the eighth century. The Judaean king Ahaz managed to preserve his kingdom and sent tribute to the Assyrians. At the end of the century his son Hezekiah would withhold tribute and revolt.[31] Apparently Hezekiah had time for planning. He expanded his line of defense westward (2 Kings 18:8), built a secure water system for the capital city (2 Kings 20:20), and erected cities and storehouses for the preservation of supplies (2 Kings 20:13; 2 Chron 32:27-30). In 701 the Assyrian king Sennacherib responded with a campaign against Judah, devastating the countryside and forcing the state to its knees. While Jerusalem itself did not fall--or at least the dynasty remained intact--the bid for a greater autonomy had failed and the price for rebellion was severe.

Internal conditions in Judah during the expansion years were likely similar to those in Israel. Those persons associated with the royal court fared much better than the average citizens. Judaean expansion required at the minimum the nucleus of a standing army, a steady source of state revenue, and a strong king. Judah may not have been as oriented toward its northern neighbors in Syria/Palestine as was Israel. Instead, it seems Judah had established some relations with Egypt (Isa 30:1-5).

While these factors are important in assessing Judah and the prophetic conflict ove property rights, perhaps the most important internal factor was the developing state administrative/judicial system

---

28   G. Rinaldi, "Quelques Remarques sur la politique d'Azarias(Ozias) de Juda en Philistie (2 Chron 26:6)," *VTSup* 9 (1962) 225-35.

29   1 Chron 5:17?

30   N. Na'aman, "Sennacherib's Letter to God on his campaign to Judah," *BASOR* 214 (1974) 25-39.

31   B. Oded, "Judah and the Exile," (*Israelite and Judaean History*, ed. Hayes and Miller), 446-47.

with its royally appointed officials. The royal initiative in appointing such officials for regional service was no doubt considered by many as a positive step. It held forth the promise of a certain uniformity in standards and a perspective wider than local bias for difficult problems. On the other hand, it is easy to understand why conflicts would develop over this system. Like all royal officials, appointees owed their allegiance first to the crown, and for this loyalty would have received the normal grants of the patronage system that accompanied such appointments. The fortified cities where the judges resided (2 Chron 19:5) also contained military commanders along with other crown officials, creating inevitable conflict between them and a local population. In fact, as noted in Chapter Three, the military leaders often times acted as judges.[32] One can understand from this reconstruction the curcial role the judicial system played in regulating local affairs and why it is closely linked to the conflict over property rights. Property must be appropriated and taxes must be levied to meet the needs of the professional security forces in the regions; also workers must be conscripted for armed and public service. When indebtedness or service obligations reached a critical level, appeal to the judiciary for help and alleviation could be disappointing. The traditional authority of the local assembly would now be overlaid and circumscribed by the authority of the appointed officials. In many cases the appointees would have been drawn from the local assembly, thus elevating a community leader above his peers. A local citizen citizen taking a case to the gate could find his/her case adjudicated by people whose interests ran against his and could manipulate the administrative machinery for their own benefit.

Some aspects of the book of Micah become clearer when seen in the light of the preceding reconstruction. The prophet's home is certainly located in the Judaean Shephelah, with *Tell Judeidah* near Beth Guvrin as the likely candidate for Moresheth-Gath.[33] His home is likely one of the fortified cities of the defensive line of the Shephelah guarding approaches to the Judaean heartland from the west, an area that played important roles in the policies of both Uzziah and Hezekiah. In any

---

[32]   Weinfeld ("Judge and Officer") finds that this sharing of personnel and offices common in other societies of the ancient Near East.

[33]   K. Elliger, "Die Heimat des Propheten Micha," *ZDPV* 57 (1934) 117-21.

reckoning, Micah's home territory was a strategic area with several key fortified cities and, according to the reconstruction given above, an area with military commanders, tax collectors, and judicial administrators.[34]

Specific oracles fit well into this background. The accusations in 2:1-2 against those who dispossess seems to presuppose legal ability to do so in spite of the value attached to the property by the victim to his *naḥalāh*. The administrative system and its manipulators are pictured in an extremely unfavorable light. Placed against a background of near martial law, these highly polemical statements are at least understandable.

Conscription appears to be the background to one of Micah's accusations. The negative effects of building Zion in 3:10 are portrayed in a general tirade against the nation's leaders.[35] Finally, the perceived oppression graphically depicted as cannibalism(3:1-3, 9-10) is attributed to the *rō'šīm* and *qāṣīn* whose titles have a clear military background,[36] and whose influential role is presupposed for state affairs.

Summary and Conclusions

The basic conclusion of this chapter can be stated in the following manner: socio-economic structure and state administrative policies in Israel and Judah were potentially oppressive, and debilitating external forces made them become so. An economy which redistributes much of the society's surplus or even necessities for the benefit of its leaders may have approval from various quarters. Such a system would, for example, better mobilize strength and leadership to fend off foreign aggression than others. Furthermore, the rights of a society's leader(s) to redistribute economic surplus and productivity coincides with a prevalent view of kingship in the ancient Near East which attributes divine initiative to the institution (cf. Ps 2; 45:1-5, 72). On the other hand, when the surplus of an economy has largely been extracted through war and forced tribute, then the tendencies toward an imbalance inherent in the rdistributing system become exacerbated. For the most

---

34   Moresheth-Gath may be the Gath of 2 Chron 11:8; so Aharoni (*Land of the Bible*, 330). Perhaps the whole list of fortified cities in 2 Chron 11:6-10, which are attributed to Rehoboam, fit better in an eighth century and later context of a Judaean military build-up.

35   Hezekiah's building projects could be in mind.

36   Judg 11:11; Josh 10:24; Isa 22:3.

part, therefore, the rich of the eighth century were those whose status was maintained through royal support and whose services were required to assist in a brief recovery from foreign domination.

Uzziah, Jotham and Jeroboam II are recorded as having carried out a census. This is not surprising since a census would be an indisensable step for rebuilding an army and the raising of revenue. A periodic census, conscription, tribute, and property appropriation were measures used by the politically agressive states upon their subjects. It seems that similar measures were "rights" exercised by Israelite and Judaean leaders as well, perhaps with increasing frequency in the eighth century and certainly with a negative perception of the consequences by the prophets. Perhaps one aspect against which the prophets reacted was the tendency to treat citizens like subjects. What an Aramaean or Assyrian ruler might demand of Israel or Judah eventually was demanded by Israelite and Judaean leaders of their people.[37]

The background reconstructed from some of Micah's accusations fits these conclusions. An emphasis on the military influence on the administrative/judicial system in Judah comes from three sources. One is the terminology employed by the prophet himself. The second is derived from the investigation of the administrative/judicial system itself(Chapter Three). The third comes from the historical circumstances behind Micah's prophecies. From the time Israel fell Judah faced Assyrian vassals on its north and west. The major entry points into Judah led through the Shephelah. A deployment of troops and fortifications in this region would have had an extensive social consequences for the property rights of citizens.

It would seem that the turmoil of the eighth century had much of the same internal tensions depicted earlier for the united monarchy; competent adjudication of citizens' concerns and fair taxation/conscription policies were also issues of the tenth century. On the other hand, the Omride period in Israel gives less evidence for social conflicts of an economic nature than either of the other periods. The conflicts appear to be primarily religious, or so the surviving sources depict them. If there is a difference, it would appear related to the international relations of the time. The Omrides had stable relations

---

[37]   The terminology for tribute to a foreign ruler and that for taxes to a native ruler is often synonymous.

with several neighbors[38] which seems to have made for general prosperity in Israel. The lack of such relations in eighth century had important consequences for the conflict over property rights.

There are two basically different sources suggested for understanding the turmoil of the eighth century. Once source is the general historical context of Israel and Judah of the period (Yahwism, Assyrian hegemony, *etc.*), and is comprised of variables whose combinations seem unique to time and place. The other source is the analysis more common to the general development of a state in the Iron Age with a redistributing economy. Other states during a similar period of development might have similar problems.[39] The prophetic perception of abused property rights derives its basis from both sources and is thus a mixture of common reactions and unique insights.

---

[38]   This assumes the Aramaean wars attributed to Ahab really belong to a later period. Cf. J. M. Miller, "The Elisha Cycle and the Accounts of the Omride Wars," *JBL* 85 (1966) 441-454; *ibid*, "The Fall of the House of Ahab," *VT* 17 (1967) 307-324.

[39]   In addition to the parallels already drawn with Neo-Assyria, one could draw a general parallel with the development of segments of Greek society: Cf. M. E. Andrews, "Hesiod and Amos," *JR* 23 (1943) 194-205; M. Detienne, *Crise agraire et attitude religieuse chez Hesiode* (Bruselles: Latomus, 1963).

Chapter Six

Conclusions

Property Rights in the eighth century prophets are usually found in the context of socio-economic conflict. There are essentially two, very similar rights at issue: (1) The right to possess immovable property(land, houses) as opposed to the right of appropriation by creditors, officials, and others; (2) The right of exacting property(taxes, usury, pledges) as opposed to the right of due process with the privilege to call certain exactions unjust. The prophets repeatedly accuse various officials as the culprits in the violation of citizens' property rights and not just the anonymous rich as popularly supposed.

There are no good reasons to assume that the prophets opposed Canaanite practices or Canaanizing officials. The culprits are assumed by the prophets to be Israelite or Judaean and their practices assumed to be(for the most part) legal and to have the authority of the state. Furthermore, there are no good reasons for assuming either state had "capitalistic" economies in the modern senses of the word. Not only is the description anachronistic and inaccurate, it also ignores the central aspect of state policies and officials who play a primary role in the conflict. Both states had economies best described as redistributing, with the initiative for direction and purpose coming from the king and his officials.

The view that a genuinely Israelite *Bodenrecht* forbade the selling of ancestral property while Canaanite principles did not was seen to be misleading. There is not enough evidence in the Hebrew Bible to prove an ethnic dualism with differing land tenure laws in Israel or Judah. Instead, an agrarian cultural pattern based on the extended family better accounts for the conservatism toward ancestral property regardless of the ethnic background of the people involved. The prophetic terminology reflected certain theological assumptions about the land; namely, it was possessed as a gift of YHWH and its misuse through graft and corruption would bring dire consequences.

In an investigation of the administrative/judicial system it was concluded that the prophetic accusations presuppose that this system and its administrators were involved in the perceived corruption affecting the property rights of citizens. By expanding the investigation to other texts, it was concluded that a state administrative/judicial system had developed in Judah(and probably in Israel too) which was staffed by royal appointees. Many of these appointees had military duties and their titles appear in both administrative/judicial texts and in the accusations of the prophets. This system played a crucial role in the protests of the prophets because its administrators' authority was not limited by local approval. The chronology of these administrative developments implies that they are an important reason for the outbreak of accusations over property rights in the eighth century.

Property rights extended to royal appointees--such as land grants and taxation privileges--contributed to the rise in land accumulation by those the prophets opposed and in the indebtedness of other citizens. This conclusion helps account for the prominent role state officials have in the prophets' accusations, even to the specific conflicts over land appropriation and exactions in kind which were the primary concerns in the latter's accusations.

One factor limiting this investigation was the comparative lack of first-hand administrative documents with which to compare the more polemical prophetical accusations. The few epigraphic remains dating to the pre-exilic period are actually quite helpful in illustrating administrative practices inferred from biblical texts, but Israelite or Judaean documents like those from ancient *Kalḫu* would be invaluable for further research. An interesting question raised by the Neo-Assyrian administrative documents concerns the possible influence from that empire upon Israel and Judah since the similarity of practices was so pronounced.

The conflict over property rights in the eighth-century prophets resulted from several factors. Primary internal factors were the privileges accorded royal officials and the developing power of the administrative/judicial system which could be used by these officials and other persons for their benefit. The primary external factor was the pressure of international relations. The attempt on the part of Israel and Judah to recover from previous political difficulties and the Assyrian influence in the whole of Syria-Palestine during the eighth century led to political and economic decisions which affected the whole economy and thus the exercise of property rights at both the national and local levels.

Bibliography

Aharoni, Y., *The Land of the Bible* (Philadelphia: Westminster Press, 1979).

_____., "The Solomonic Districts," *TA* 3 (1976) 5-15.

_____., "The Use of Hieratic Numerals in Hebrew Ostraca and the Shekel Weights," *BASOR* 184 (1966) 13-19.

Albright, W. F., "The Judicial Reform of Jehoshaphat," *Alexander Marx Jubilee Volume* (ed. S. Lieberman; Philadelphia: Jewish Publication Society 1950) 61-82.

Allen, L., *Joel, Obadiah, Jonah and Micah* (NICOT; Grand Rapids: Eerdmans, 1976).

Alt, A., "Der Anteil des Konigtum an der sozialen Entwicklung in den Reichen Israel und Juda," *Kleine Schriften zur Geschichte des Volkes Israels* (3 vols; Münich: C. H. Beck 'she, 1953-59) 3. 348-72.

_____., "Micha 2, 1-5. *Ges Anadasmos* in Juda," *Kleine Schriften* 3. 373-81.

_____., "The Origins of Israelite Law," *Essays on Old Testament History and Religion* (Graden City: Doubleday & Co., 1966) 103-71.

_____., "Der Stadstaat Samaria," *Kleine Schriften* 3. 258-302.

Andersen, K. T., "Die Chronologie der Könige von Israel und Juda," *ST* 23 (1969) 67-112.

Andrews, M. E., "Hesiod und Amos," *JR* 23 (1943) 194-205.

Asheri, D., "Laws of Inheritance, Distribution of Land and Political Constitutions in Ancient Greece," *Historia* 12 (1963) 1-21.

Astour, M., "The First Assyrian Invasion of Israel," *JAOS* 91 (1971) 383-89.

Austin, M. & Vidal-Naquet, P., *Economic and Social History of Ancient Greece* (Berkeley: University of California Press, 1977).

Avigad, N., "New Light on the Na'ar Seals," *Magnalia Dei* (ed. F. M. Cross et al; Garden City: Doubleday & Co., 1976) 294-300

Bach, R., "Gottesrecht und weltlichen Recht in der Verkündigung des Propheten Amos," *Festschrift fur Gunther Dehn* (ed. W. Schneemelcher; Neukirchen: Neukirchener Verlag, 1957) 23-34.

Bächli, R., *Amphiktyonie im Alten Testament* (TZ6; Basel: Friedrich Reinhardt, 1977).

Bardtke, Hans, "Die Latifundien in Juda wahrend der zweiten Halfte des achten Jahrhunderts v. Chr (Zum Verstandnis von Jes 5, 8-10)," in *Hommages a Andre Dupont-Sommer* (ed. A. Caquot; Paris: Librairie Adrien Maison-neuve, 1971) 235-54.

Bartlett, John, *Amos's Oracles against the Nations* (SOTSMS 6; Cambridge: Cambridge University Press, 1980).

Batto, B., "Land Tenure and Women at Mari," *JESHO* 23 (1980) 210-32.

Beek, M. A., "The Religious Background of Amos 2:6-8,"*OTS* 5 (1948) 132-41.

Bergren, R., *The Prophets and the Law* (Cincinnati: Hebrew Union Press, 1974).

Bess, S. H., *Systems of Land Tenure In Ancient Israel* (unpublished dissertation; University of Michigan, 1963).

Beyerlin, W., *Die Kulttradition Israels in der Verkündigung des Propheten Micha* (FRLANT 54; Göttingen: Vandenhoeck & Ruprecht, 1959).

_____., *Near Eastern Religious Texts Relating to the Old Testament* (Philadelphia: Westminster Press, 1978).

Biran, A., "Tel Dan---- 5 Years Later," *BA* 43 (1980) 168-82.

Birch, B., *The Rise of the Israelite Monarchy: The Growth and Development of I Samuel 7-15* (SBLDS 27; Missoula: Scholars Press, 1976).

Boecker, H. J., *Redeformen des Rechtsleben im Alten Testament* (WMANT 14; Neukirchen: Neukirchener Verlag, 1964).

Bohlen, R., *Der Fall Nabot* (TTS 35; Trier: Paulinus-Verlag, 1978).

Bolle, W., *Das israelitische Bodenrecht* (theological dissertation; Berlin, 1929).

Box, G. H., "Amos 2:6 and 8:6," *Exp Tim* 12 (1900-01) 377-78.

Boyer, G., "La place des textes d'Ugarit dans l"historie de L'ancien droit oriental," in J. Nougayrol, ed., *Le palais royal d' Ugarit, III* (Mission de Ras Shamra VI; Paris: Imprimerie Nationale, 1955) 200-305.

_____., *Textes Juridiques* (ARM VIII; Paris: Imprimerie Nationale, 1958).

Buccellati, G., *Cities and Nations of Ancient Syria* (Studi Semitici 26; Rome: University of Rome, 1967).

Buss, M., "The Social Psychology of Prophecy," *Prophecy. Essays presented to Georg Fohrer* (BZAW 150; Berlin: de Gruyter, 1980) 1-11.

Carney. T. F., *The Economics of Antiquity* (Lawrence: Coronado Press, 1973).

Causse, A., *Du groupe ethnique a la communauté religeuse; le problem sociologique de la religion d'Israel* (Paris: Felix Alcan, 1937).

Childs, B., *The Book of Exodus* (OTL; Philadelphia: Westminster, 1974).

Christensen, D., *Transformations of the War Oracle in Old Testament Prophecy* (HDR 3; Missoula: Scholars Press, 1975).

Clements, R. E., "The Deuteronomistic Interpretation of the Founding of the Monarchy in I Samuel VIII," *VT* 24 (1974) 398-410.

Cogan, M., *Imperialism and Religion: Assyria, Judah and Israel in the Eighth and Seventh Centuries B. C. E.* (SBLMS 19; Missoula: Scholars Press, 1974).

Cohen, H. R., *Biblical Hapax Legomena in the Light of Akkadian and Ugaritic* (SBLDS 37; Missoula: Scholars Press, 1978).

Cohen, M. A., "The Prophets as Revolutionaries: A Socio-Political Analysis," *BAR* 5 (1979) 12-19.

Cornill, C. H., *The Prophets of Israel* (Chicago: Open Court, 1913).

Crenshaw, J. L., "The Influence of the Wise Upon Amos," *ZAW* 79, (1967) 42-51.

Crowfoot, J. W., K. Kenyon, E. L. Sukenik, *The Buildings at Samaria* (Samaria-Sebaste I; London: Palestine Exploration Fund, 1942).

Crüsemann, F., *Der Widerstand gegen das Konigtum* (WMANT 49; Neukirchen: Neukirchener Verlag, 1978).

Dalton, G., ed., *Tribal and Peasant Economics* (Garden City: Natural History Press, 1967).

Dietrich, W., *Israel und Kanaan* (SBS 94; Stuttgart: Katholisches Bibelwerk. 1979).

Donner, H., "Die soziale Botschaft des Propheten im Lichte der Gesellschaftsordnung in Israel," *Or Ant* 2 (1963) 229-45.

_____., *Studien zur Verfassungs-und Verwaltungsgeschichte der Reiche Israel und Juda* (dissertation; Leipzig, 1956).

Driel, van G., "Land and People in Assyria," *BiOr* 27 (1970) 168-75.

Duhm, B., *Jesaja* (HAT; Göttingen: Vandenhoeck & Ruprecht, 1902).

_____., *Die Theologie der Propheten als Grundlage fur die innere Entwicklungsgeschichte der israelitischen Religion* (Bonn: Adolph Marcus, 1875).

Eissfeldt, O., *Erstlinge und Zehnten im Alten Testament* (BWANT 1/22; Stuttgart: Kolhammer, 1917).

_____., *The Old Testament. An Introduction* (Oxford: Basil Blackwell, 1965).

Ekholm, K. and J. Friedman, "'Capital' Imperialism and Exploitation in Ancient World Empires," *Power and Propaganda. A Symposium on Ancient Empires* (Mesopotamia 7; ed. M. Trolle Larsen; Copenhagen: Akademisk Forlag, 1979) 41-58.

Elliger, K., "Die Heimat des Propheten Micha," *ZDPV* 57 (1934) 81-152.

Fales, F. M., *Censimenti e catasti di epoca neoassira* (Studie economici e tecnoligici 2; Rome: University of Rome, 1973).

Fendler, M., "Zur Sozialkritik des Amos," *EvT* 33 (1973) 32-53.

Fensham, F. C., "Common Trends in Curses of the Near Eastern Treaties and KUDURRU-Inscriptions Compared with Maledictions of Amos and Isaiah," *ZAW* 75 (1963) 155-75.

_____., "Widow, Orphan and the Poor in Ancient Near East Legal and Wisdom Literature," *JNES* 21 (1962) 129-39.

Fey, R., *Amos und Jesaja. Abhangigkeit und Eigenstandigkeit des Jesaja* (WMANT 12; Neukirchen: Neukirchener Verlag, 1963).

Finley, M. I., "The Alienability of Land in Ancient Greece," *Eirene* 7 (1968) 25-32.

_____., *Problemes de la terre en Grece ancienne* (Netherlands: The Hague, 1973).

Fohrer, G., *Das Buch Jesaja* (Zurich: Zwingli Verlag, 1960).

_____., "Zur Einwirkung der gesellschaftlichen Struktur Israels auf seine Religion," *Near Eastern Studies in honor of W. F. Albright* (ed. H. Goedicke; Baltimore: Johns Hopkins, 1971) 169-85.

Forshey, H. O., *The Hebrew Root NHL and its Semitic Cognates* (unpublished dissertation, Harvard University, 1973).

Frankenstein, S., "The Phoenicians in the Far West: A Function of New-Assyrian Imperialism," *Power and Propagamda. A symposium on Ancient Empires* (Mesopotamia 7; ed. M. Trolle Larsen; Copenhagen: Akademisk Forlag, 1979) 263-94.

Frick, F., *The City in Ancient Israel* (SBLDS 36; Missoula: Scholars Press, 1977).

Gamoran, H., "The Biblical Law Against Loans on Interest," *JNES* 30 (1971) 127-34.

Gelston, A., "Kingship in the book of Hosea," *OTS* 19 (1974) 71-85.

Gerstenberger, E., *Wesen und Herkunft des "Apodiktischen Rechts"* (WMANT 20; Neukirchen: Neukirchener Verlag, 1965).

_____., "The Woe Oracles of the Prophets," *JBL* 81 (1962) 249-63.

Gesenius, W., *Hebrew and Chaldee Lexicon* (Grand Rapids: Eerdmans, 1949).

Geva, S., "A Reassessment of the Chronology of Beth Shean Stratum V and IV," *IEJ* 20 (1979) 6-10.

Goetze, A., *Kleinasien* (KAO III/1; München: Beck, 1957).

Gottwald, N., *The Tribes of Yahweh* (Maryknoll: Orbis Books, 1979).

Graham, W. C., *The Prophets and Israel's Culture* (Chicago: University of Chicago Press, 1934).

Gray, G. B., *Isaiah 1-27* (ICC; New York: Charles Scribner's Sons, 1912).

_____., *Numbers* (ICC; New York: Charles Scribner's Sons, 1963).

Gray, J., "Feudalism in Ugarit and Early Israel," *ZAW* 64 (1952) 49-55.

Hammershaimb, E., "On the Ethics of the Old Testament Prophets," *VTSup* 7 (1960) 75-101.

_____., "Some Leading Ideas in the Book of Micah," *Some Aspects of Old Testament Prophecy from Isaiah to Malachi* (Copenhagen: Rosenkilde og Bagger, 1966) 29-50.

Haran, M., "The Rise and Decline of the Empire of Jeroboam ben Joash," *VT* 17 (1967) 267-84.

Hardmeier, C., *Texttheorie und biblische Exegese: zur rhetorischen Funktion der Trauermetaphorik in der Prophetie* (BET 79; Münich: Chr. Kaiser, 1978).

Harper, W. R., *Amos & Hosea* (ICC; New York: Charles Scribner's Sons, 1905).

Hayes, J. H., "The History of the Form-Critical Study of Prophecy," *SBLSP* (ed. G. MacRae; Missoula: Scholars Press, 1973) 1. 60-99.

Heltzer, M., *The Rural Community in Ancient Ugarit* (Wiesbaden: Ludwig Reichert Verlag, 1976).

Henrey, K. H., "Land Tenure in the Old Testament," *PEQ* 86 (1954) 5-15.

Hentschke, R., *Satzung und Setzender* (BWANT 3; Stuttgart: W. Kolhammer, 1963).

Herr, L. G., *The Scripts of Ancient North West Semitic Seals* (Missoula: Scholars Press, 1978).

Herrmann, S., *A History of Israel in Old Testament Times* (Philadelphia: Fortress Press, 1975).

Holladay, J. S., "Assyrian Statecraft and the Prophets of Israel," *HTR* 63 (1970) 29-51.

Holm-Nielsen, S., "Die Sozialkritik der Propheten," *Denkender Glaube* (ed. O. Kaiser; Berlin: de Gruyter, 1976) 7-23.

Irwin, W. A., "The Thinking of Amos," *AJSL* 49 (1932/33) 102-114.

Ishida, T., "The Leaders of the Tribal Leagues 'Israel,'" *RB* 80 (1973) 514-30.

Jackson, B. S., "Liability for Intention in Early Jewish Law," *Essays in Jewish and Comparative Legal History* (SJLA 10; Leiden: E. J. Brill, 1975) 202-34.

_____., *Theft in Early Jewish Law* (Oxford: Clarendon Press, 1972).

Janzen, W., *Mourning Cry and Woe Oracle* (BZAW 125; Berlin: de Gruyter, 1972).

Jean, D. F. and J. Hoftizer, *Dictionnaire des inscriptions semitiques de l'ouest* (Leiden: E. J. Brill, 1965).

Jeppesen, K., "New Aspects of Micah Research," *JSOT* 8 (1978) 3-32.

Johnson, A. R., "The Primary Meaning of G'L," *VTSup* 1 (1953) 67-77.

Junge, E., *Der Wiederaufbau des Heerwesens der Reiches Juda unter Josia* (BWANT 75; Stuttgart: Kolhammer Verlag, 1937).

Kaiser, O., "Gerechtigkeit und Heil," *NZSyTh* 11 (1969) 312-28.

_____., *Isaiah 1-12* (OTL; Philadelphia: Westminster Press, 1972).

Kenyon, K., *Archaeology in the Holy Land* (New York: W. W. Norton, 1979).

_____., *Royal Cities of the Old Testament* (London: Barric & Jenkins, 1971).

Kirkpatrick, A. F., *Doctrine of the Prophets* (London: Macmillan & Co., 1932).

Knierim, R., "Exodus 18 und die Neuordnung der mosaischen Gerichtsbarkeit," *ZAW* 73 (1961) 146-71.

Koch, K., "Die Entstehung der sozialen Kritik bei den Profeten," *Probleme Biblischer Theologie* (ed. H. W. Wolff; Münich: Chr. Kaiser, 1971) 236-57.

Köhler, L., *Hebrew Man* (Nashville: Abingdon Press, 1956).

Kraus, H. J., "Die Prophetische Botschaft gegen das soziale Unrecht Israels," *EvT* 15 (1955) 295-307.

Kuenen, A., *The Prophets and Prophecy in Israel* (London: Longmans, Green & Co., 1877).

Kuschke, A., "Arm und reich im Alten Testament mit besonder Berucksichtigung der nachexilischen Zeit," *ZAW* 59 (1939) 31-57.

Lachmann, E. R., "Note on Ruth 4:7-8," *JBL* 56 (1937) 53-56.

Lance, H. D., "Royal Stamps and the Kingdom of Judah," *HTR* 72 (1971) 315-32.

Lapp, P., "Late Royal Seals from Judah," *BASOR* 158 (1960) 11-22.

Larsen, M. Trolle, "The Tradition of Empre in Mesopotamia," *Power & Propaganda. A symposium on Ancient Empires* (Mesopotamia 7; ed. M. Trolle Larsen; Copenhagen: Akademisk Forlag, 1979) 75-103.

Lemaire, A., *Inscriptions Hebraiques* (LAPO; Paris: Cerf, 1977).

Lewy, H., "The Nuzian Feudal System," *Or* 11 (1942) 1-40, 209-50, 297-349.

Lipinski, E., "An Assyro-Israelite Alliance in 842/41 B. C. E." *Sixth World Congress of Jewish Studies* (Jerusalem: Academic Press, 1977) 273-78.

Loretz, O., "Die prophetische Kritik des Rentenkapitalismus," *UF* 7 (1975) 271-78.

Lurje, M., *Studien zur Geschichte der Wirtschaftlicher und social Verhältnisse im Israelitische-Judische Reiche* (BZAW 45; Giessen: A. Topel-mann, 1927).

McClellan, T., "Towns and Fortresses: The Transformation of Urban Life in Judah from 8th to 7th Centuries B. C.," *SBLSP* (ed. P. Achtemeier; Missoula: Scholars Press, 1978) 1. 277-85.

McKenzie, D., "Judicial Procedure at the town gate," *VT* 14 (1964) 100-104.

McKenzie, J. L., "The Elders in the Old Testament," *Bib* 40 (1959) 522-40.

Maag, V., *Text, Wortshütz und Begriffswelt des Buches Amos* (Leiden: E. J. Brill, 1951).

Macholz, G., "Die Stellung des Konigs in der israelitischen Gerichtsverfassung," *ZAW* 84 (1972) 157-82.

_____., "Zur Geschichte der Justizorganization in Juda," *ZAW* 84 (1972) 314-40.

Malamat, A., "The Aramaeans," *Peoples of Old Testament Times* (ed. D. J. Wiseman; Oxford: The Clarendon Press, 1973) 134-55.

_____., "Mari and the Bible: Some Patterns of Tribal Organization and Institutions," JAOS (1962) 143-50.

Mallowan, M., "Samaria and Calah-Nimrud: Conjunctions in History and Archaeology," *Archaeology in the Levant. Essays for Kathleen Kenyon* (ed. R. Moorey and P. Parr; Warminster: Aris & Phillips, 1978) 155-63.

Maloney, R. P., "Usury and Restrictions on Interest-Taking in the Ancient Near East," *CBQ* 36 (1974) 1-20.

March E., "Prophecy," in *Old Testament Form Criticism* (ed. J. H. Hayes; San Antonio: Trinity University Press, 1974) 141-78.

Marmorstein, E., "The Origins of Agricultural Feudalism in the Holy Land," *PEQ* 85 (1953) 11-17.

Mauchline, J., *1 and 2 Samuel* (NCB; London: Oliphants, 1971).

Mayes, A. D. H., *Deuteronomy* (NCB; London: Oliphants, 1979).

Mays, J., *Amos* (OTL; Philadelphia: Westminster Press, 1969).

_____., *Hosea* (OTL; Philadelphia: Westminster Press, 1969).

_____., *Micah* (OTL; Philadelphia: Westminster Press, 1976).

Mazar, B., "The Military Elite of King David," *VT* 13 (1963) 310-20.

_____., "The Cities of the Priests and Levites," *VTSup* 7 (1960) 193-205.

Mendelsohn, I., "Samuel's Denunciation of Kingship in Light of the Akkadian Documents from Ugarit," *BASOR* 143 (1956) 17-22.

_____., *Slavery in the Ancient Near East* (New York: Oxford University Press, 1949).

Mettinger, T. N. D., *Solomonic State Officials. A Study of the Civil Government Officials of the Israelite Monarchy* (CB, OTS 5; Lund: CWK Gleerup, 1971).

Miller, J. M., "The Elisha Cycle and the Accounts of the Omride Wars," *JBL* 85 (1966) 441-54.

_____., *The Omride Dynasty in the Light of Recent Literary and Archaeological Research* (unpublished dissertation, Emory University, 1964).

_____., "Saul's Rise to Power: Some Observations Concerning I Sam 9:1 - 10:16; 10:26 - 11:15," *CBQ* 36 (1974) 157-74.

Morgenstern, J., "Amos Studies (Part IV)," *HUCA* 32 (1961) 295-350.

Na'aman, N., "Sennacherib's Campaign to Judah and the date of the *'lmlk'* stamps," *VT* 29 (1979) 71-86.

_____., "Sennacherib's 'Letter to God' on his campaign to Judah," *BASOR* 214 (1974) 25-39.

Nash, M., *Primitive and Peasant Economic Systems* (San Francisco: Chandler, 1966).

Naveh, J., "A Hebrew Letter from the Seventh Century B. C.," *IEJ* 10 (1960) 129-39.

Neufeld, E., "The Emergence of a royal-urban Society in Ancient Israel," *HUCA* 31 (1960) 31-53.

_____., "The Prohibition Against Loans at Interest in Ancient Hebrew Laws," *HUCA* 26 (1955) 355-412.

North, R., *Sociology of the Biblical Jubilee* (AnBib 4; Rome: Pontifical Biblical Institute, 1954).

Noth, M., "Das Amt des 'Richters Israels,'" *Gesammelte Studien zum Alten Testament* (TBü 39; München: Chr. Kaiser, 1969).

_____., *Exodus* (OTL; Philadelphia: Westminster Press, 1962).

_____., *Numbers* (OTL; Philadlphia: Westminster Press, 1966).

_____., "Das Krongut der israelitischen Könige und seine Verwaltung," *ZDPV* 40 (1927) 211-44.

_____., "Office and Vocation in the Old Testament," *The Laws in the Pentateuch and other Studies* (Philadelphia: Fortress Press, 1967) 229-49.

_____., *Das System der zwölf Stämme Israels* (BWANT 1; Stuttgart: Kolhammer Verlag, 1930).

_____., *Uberlieferungsgeschichtliche Studien* (Tübingen: Max Niemeyer, 1957).

Nowack, D. W., *Die kleinen Propheten* (HAT; Göttingen: Vandenhoeck & Ruprecht, 1897).

Nystrom, S., *Beduinentum und Jahwismus* (Lund: CWK Cleerup, 1946).

Oded, B., "Judah and the Exile," *Israelite and Judaean History* (ed. J. Hayes and J. M. Miller; Philadelphia: Westminster Press, 1977) 435-88.

Oden, R., "Hermeneutics and Historiography: Germany and America," *SBLSP* (ed. P. Achtemeier, 1980) 135-58.

Oyen, H. van, *Ethik des Alten Testaments* (Gütersloh: Gerd Mohn, 1967).

Pardee, D., "The Judicial Plea from Mesad Hashavyahu (Yavneh Yam): A New Philological Study," *Maarav* 1 (1978-79) 33-66.

Patrick, D., "Casuistic Law Governing Primary Rights and Duties," *JBL* 92 (1973) 180-84.

Paul S. and W. Dever, *Biblical Archaeology* (New York: Quadrangle, 1974).

Peckham, B., "Israel and Phoenicia," *Magnalia Dei* (ed. F. M. Cross et al; Garden City: Doubleday & Co., 1976) 224-48.

Phillips, A., *Ancient Israel's Criminal Law* (Oxford: Basil Blackwell, 1970).

Ploeg, J. van der, "Les soterim d'Israel," *OTS* 10 (1954) 185-96.

Ploger, J., *Literarkritische, Formgeschichtliche und Stilkritische Untersuchung zum Deuteronomium* (BBB 26; Bonn: Peter Hanstein, 1967).

Polanyi, K., *Trade and Market in the early Empires: Economics in History and Theory* (Chicago: The Free Press, 1957).

Porteous, N., "The Basis of the Ethical Teaching of the Prophets," *Studies in Old Testament Prophecy* (ed. H. H. Rowley; New York: Charles Scribner's Sons, 1950) 143-56.

Postgate, J. N., *The Governor's Palace Archive* (London: The British School of Archaeology in Iraq, 1973).

_____., *New Assyrian Royal Grants and Decrees* (Rome: Pontifical Biblical Institute, 1969).

_____., "Some Remarks on Conditions in the Assyrian Countryside," *JESHO* 17 (1974) 225-43.

_____., *Taxation and Conscription in the Assyrian Empire* (Rome: Biblical Institute Press, 1974).

_____., "The Economic Structure of the Assyrian Empire," *Power and Propaganda. A symposium on Ancient Empires* (Mesopotamia 7; ed. M. Trolle Larsen; Copenhagen: Akademisk Forlag, 1979) 193-221.

Purves, P. M., "Commentary on Nuzi Real Property in the Light of Recent Studies," *JNES* 4 (1945) 68-86.

Rad, G. von, *Deuteronomy* (OTL; Philadelphia: Westminster Press, 1966).

_____., *Old Testament Theology* (New York: Harper & Row, 1965).

_____., "The Promised Land and Yahweh's Land in the Hexateuch," *The Problem of the Hexateuch and Other Essays* (New York: McGraw Hill, 1966) 79-93,

Rainey, A., "Administration in Ugarit and the Samaria Ostraca," *IEJ* 12 (1962) 62-63.

_____., "The Samaria Ostraca in the Light of Fresh Evidence," *PEQ* 99 (1967) 32-41.

_____., "The Sitz in Leben of the Samaria Ostraca," *TA* 6 (1979) 90-94.

_____., *The Social Stratification of Ugarit* (unpublished dissertation, Brandeis University, 1962).

_____., "The System of Land Grants at Ugarit in Its Wider Near Eastern Setting," *Fourth World Congress of Jewish Studies* (Jerusalem: World Congress of Jewish Studies, 1967). 1. 187-91.

Reisner, G. A. et al., *Harvard Excavations at Samaria 1908-10* (Cambridge: Harvard University Press, 1924).

Reventlow, H. G., *Das Amt der Propheten bei Amos* (FRLANT 80; Göttingen: Vandenhoeck and Ruprecht, 1962).

Reviv, H., "Some Comments on the Maryannu," *IEJ* 22 (1972) 218-28.

Richter, W., "Zu den 'Richtern Israels,'" *ZAW* 77 (1965) 40-72.

Robinson, T. H., *Die Zwölf Kleinen Propheten* (HAT 14; Tübingen: J. C. B. Mohr, 1954).

_____., "Some Economic and Social Factors in the History of Israel," *Exp Tim* 45 (1933-34) 264-260, 294-300.

Rosenbloom, J. R., "Social Science Concepts of Modernization and Biblical History: The Development of the Israelite Monarchy," *JAAR* 40 (1972) 437-444.

Rowley, H. H., "The Marriage of Ruth,:" *The Servant of the Lord and Other Essays* (London: Lutterworth Press, 1952) 161-86.

Rudolph, W., *Chronikbücher* (HAT 21; Tübingen: J. C. B. Mohr, 1955).

_____., *Hosea* (KAT 13/2; Gütersloh: Gerd Mohn, 1971).

_____., *Joel-Amos-Obadja-Jona* (KAT 13/2; Gütersloh: Gerd Mohn, 1971).

_____., *Micha-Nahum-Habakuk-Zephanje* (KAT 13/3; Gütersloh: Gerd Mohn, 1975).

Salmon, J. D., *Judicial Authority in Early Israel* (unpublished dissertation, Princeton Theological Seminary, 1968).

Sarna, N., "Zedekiah's Emancipation of Slaves and the Sabbatical Year," *Orient and Occident* (AOAT 22; ed. H. Hoffner, 1973) 143-49.

Sasson, V., "An Unrecognized Juridical Term in the Yabneh-Yam Lawsuit and in an Unnoticed Biblical Parallel,: *BASOR* 232 (1978) 57-64.

Schwantes, M., *Das Recht der Armen* (BET 4; Frankfort: Peter Lang, 1977).

Scott, B. Y., *The Relevance of the Prophets* (New York: Macmillan, 1944).

Seeligmann, I. L., "Zur Terminologie fur das Gerichtsverfahren im Wortschatz des biblischen Hebraische," *Hebraische Wortforschung* (VTSup 16) 251-78.

Seitz, G., *Redaktionsgeschichtliche Studien zum Deuteronomium* (BWANT 93; Stuttgart: W. Kolhammer, 1971) 200-02.

Sellin, E., *Das Zwölfprophetenbuch* (KAT 12/1; Leipzig: A. Deitchert, 1929).

Selms, A. van, "Jubilee Year," *IDBS* (Nashville: Abindgon Press, 1976) 496-98.

_____., *Marriage and Family Life in Ugaritic Literature* (London: Luzac & Co., 1954).

Smith, J. M. Powis, *The Prophets and Their Times* (Chicago: University of Chicago Press, 1940).

Smith, W. R., *Lectures on the Religion of the Semites* (Edinburgh: A. & C. Black, 1894).

Speiser, E. A., "Of Shoes and Shekels," *BASOR* 77 (1940) 15-20.

Steck, O. H., "Die Gesellschaftskritik der Propheten," *Christentum und Gesellschaft* (ed. B. Lohse et al.; Göttingen: Vandenhoeck & Ruprecht, 1969).

Stoebe, H. J., *Das Erste Buch Samuelis* (KAT 8/1; Gütersloh: Gerd Mohn, 1973).

Sulzberger, M., "Status of Labor in Ancient Israel,: *JQR* 13 (1922-23) 245-302, 397-459.

Tadmor, H. and A. R. Millard, "Adad Nirari III in Syria," *Iraq* 35 (1973) 57-64.

_____., "Assyria and the West: The Ninth Century and Its Aftermath," *Unity and Diversity. Essays in the History, Literature, and Religion of the Ancient Near East* (ed. H. Goedicke and J. J. M. Roberts; Baltimore: Johns Hopkins, 1975) 36-48.

Talmon, S., "The Gezer Calendar and the Seasonal Cycle of Ancient Canaan," *JAOS* 83 (1963) 177-87.

Thompson, R. M., *Penitence and Sacrifice in Early Israel Outside the Levitical Law* (Leiden: E. J. Brill, 1963).

Thompson, T. & D., "Some Legal Problems in the Book of Ruth," *VT* 18 (1968) 79-99.

Troeltsch, E., "Glaube und Ethos der hebraischen Propheten," *Aufsätze zur Geistesgeschichte und Religionssoziologie* (Gesammelte Schriften 4; Tübingen: J. C. B. Mohr, 1925) 34-65.

Ussishkin, D., "The Destruction of Lachish by Sennacherib and the Dating of the Royal Judean Storage Jars," *TA* 4 (1977) 28-60.

Vaux, R. de, *Ancient Israel* (New York: McGraw Hill, 1965) 2.

Waard, J. de, "The Chiastic Structure of Amos 5:1-17," *VT* 27 (1977) 170-77.

Waldow, E. von, "Social Responsibility and Social Structure in Early Israel," *CBQ* 32 (1970) 182-204.

Walter, F., *Die Propheten in ihren sozialen Beruf und das Wirtschaftsleben ihren Zeit* (Freiburg: Breisgau, 1900).

Wanke, G., "Zu Grundlagen und Absicht prophetischer Sozialkritik,: *KD* 18 (1972) 2-17.

Warmuth, G., *Das Mahnwort* (BET 1; Frankfurt: Peter Lang, 1976).

Weber, M., *The Agrarian Sociology of Ancient Civilizations* (London: NLB, 1976).

_____., *Ancient Judaism* (Glencoe: The Free Press, 1952).

Weinfeld, M., *Deuteronomy and the Deuteronomic School* (Oxford: Clarendon Press, 1972).

_____., "Judge and Officer in the Ancient Near East and In Ancient Israel," *IOS* 7 (1977) 65-88.

Wellhausen, J., *Die Composition des Hexateuchs und der historischen Bücher des Alten Testaments* (Berlin: Georg Reimer, 1889).

_____., *Israelitische und Jüdische Geschichte* (Berlin: de Gruyter, 1958).

_____., *Die Kleinen Propheten* (Berlin: de Gruyter, 1963).

_____., *Prolegomena to the History of Israel* (New York: Meridian, 1957).

Welten, P., *Die Konigs-Stempel* (Wiesbaden: Otto Harrassowitz, 1969).

Westermann, C., B*asic Forms of Prophetic Speech* (Philadelphia: Westminster Press, 1967).

Whedbee, J. W., *Isaiah and Wisdom* (Nashville: Abindgon Press, 1971).

Whitelam, K. W., *The Just King* (JSOTS 12; Sheffield: JSOT Press, 1979).

Whitley, C. F., *The Prophetic Achievement* (Leiden: E. J. Brill, 1963).

Wildberger, H., *Jesaja* (BKAT 10; Neukirchen: Neukirchener Verlag, 1972).

Wilson, J. V. Kinnier, *The Nimrud Wine Lists. A study of men and administration at the Assyrian Capital in the Eighth Century, B. C.* (London: The British School of Archaeology in Iraq, 1973).

Wiseman, D. J., "Alalakh," *Archaeology and Old Testament Study* (ed. D. W. Thomas; Oxford: The Clarendon Press, 1967) 119-35.

_____., *The Alalakh Tablets* (London: British Institute of Archaeology at Ankara, 1953).

Wolff, H. W., *Amos and Joel* (Hermeneia; Philadelphia: Fortress Press, 1977).

_____., *Amos' geistige Heimat* (WMANT 18; Neukirchen: Neukirchener Verlag, 1964).

_____., "Micah the Moreshite---- The Prophet and His Background," *Israelite Wisdom: Theological and Literary Essays in Honor of Samuel Terrien* (ed. J. G. Gammie *et al*; New York: Union Theological Seminary, 1978) 77-84.

_____., "'Wissen um Gott' bei Hosea als Urform der Theologie," *EvT* 12 (1952-53) 533-54.

Woude, A. van der, "Micah in Dispute with the Pseudo-Prophets," *VT* 19 (1969) 244-60.

Wright, G. E., "The Provinces of Solomon," *EI* 9 (1967) 58-68.

Wright, T. J., "Did Amos Inspect Livers?" *ABR* 23 (1975) 3-11.

_____., "Amos and the 'Sycamore Fig,'" *VT* 26 (1976) 362-68.

Würthwein, E., "Amos Studien," *ZAW* 62 (1950) 10-52.

Yadin, Y., "The Fourfold Division of Judah," *BASOR* 163 (1961) 6-12.

_____., "Recipients or Owners. A Note on the Samaria Ostraca," *IEJ* 9 (1959) 184-87.

Zaccagnini, C., "The Price of the Fields at Nuzi," *JESHO* 22 (1979) 1-32

Zimmerli, W., *The Law and the Prophets* (Oxford: Basil Blackwell, 1965).